The Fabulous Fantora Files

Adèle Geras

D0488743

OXFORD
UNIVERSITY PRESS

Introduction

I am an expert on the Fantora family. I am the Keeper
of the Files, although no one in the family talks about
them very much. Perhaps they don't like to dwell on
the fact that all their secrets, thoughts and feelings (as
well as everything they do, of course) are on record.
I am the guardian of the family history. A bit of an
unlikely guardian, I can hear you say. Whoever heard
of a cat talking, let alone writing things down? Well,
I *can* talk and write and have been able to for a very
long time. As a matter of fact, the entire Fantora
family is somewhat strange, as you will see. My name
is Ozymandias – I like it. It comes from a poem.
The whole line is: 'My name is Ozymandias, King
of Kings', which has a splendid ring to it. Whenever
I pass a mirror, I say to my reflection: 'My name is
Ozymandias, cat of cats' – only a very small variation
on the original – and it always gives me pleasure.
The family call me Ozzy. This is a liberty I allow them.
Francesca started it. You'd think, of all people,
she'd know better. She's nearly six, but even at such
a tender age, she has a mind of her own. She is an

even-tempered, delightful little girl in every possible way, but she will not have her name shortened. Francesca is what she is called, however inconvenient. Say 'Fran', 'Franny', 'Cesca', and worst of all, 'Chess', ('I'm not a game, am I?' she asks, and quite right too) and you will see the sparks fly. Literally. She stamps her dainty foot and blue flames leap up from the toes of her shoes. On her first day at school, she very nearly set fire to the Library Corner. Certainly two or three books were so badly singed that they couldn't even be given to the Harvest Jumble Sale.

How do I know this when I wasn't there? I know everything. Well, perhaps not quite everything, and not everything in the whole wide world, but certainly all about the Fantoras, even when they're out of my sight. As you will see when I begin my story – or stories, for there are quite a number of them – I can put down other people's innermost thoughts and feelings, conversations that have taken place miles away, and detailed descriptions of houses I have never visited in the furry flesh. This is because, as well as being the Keeper of the Files, I am also a Narrator. That is a magical being who can tell you everything and take you everywhere without stirring from his cushion by the fire. In my case, it's a combination of intelligence, imagination, and a dollop of secret powers, passed on to me by my Egyptian ancestors.

Let us begin then with the morning the whole Fantora family had their picture in the local newspaper. The reason for the picture was very sad indeed. The Fantora family home, known as Turrets, had burned to the ground the week before, and we were all staying at the Belmont Private Hotel, waiting to move to a square, newly-built house on Azalea Avenue, which is part of the Barton Bridge Estate. The picture showed us all (yes, even I was in it!) standing forlornly about in a dazed condition worrying about our belongings. From left to right, then, there we were; Bianca (aged 10), Francesca (aged 5), Marco (aged 9), Edward their father (always called Eddie), Rosamund their mother (always called Rosie), Filomena their grandmother, and Varvara, their aunt. Yes, it *is* Varvara and not Barbara ever since Auntie Varvara learned that this was the Eastern European spelling of her name. I am standing to the right of the picture, looking grumpy. My name is not given, but I'm used to that.

'You'd think,' said Auntie Varvara, as we all pored over the newspaper during breakfast that morning, 'that they'd say a little more, wouldn't you? It's a bit abrupt, isn't it: "Local family burned out. The Veggie Burger

5

Disaster." I do wish they didn't have to call it that.'

'Well,' said Marco, 'it *was* your veggie burgers that caught fire. Fancy leaving them frying and then forgetting about them and going out.'

'I was going to my yoga class,' said Auntie Varvara.

'Then why did you put the veggie burgers on to cook?' said Eddie.

Auntie Varvara sighed and helped herself to the branflakes. 'I forgot about my yoga class and started cooking. Then I went out of the kitchen and forgot the burgers and remembered my class, so off I went, and then ...' Auntie Varvara started crying quietly.

'Stop that at once,' said Filomena, who is always called Filomena, and never, ever Granny. 'There's no need to cry. And there's no need for the rest of you to bully her. Her absent-mindedness is a consequence of her vegetarianism. I always said no good would come of it. Red blood, that's what's required. If I've said it once, I've said it a thousand times.'

'I agree with vegetarianism,' said Bianca.

'Me too,' said Marco, chomping on his kippers.

'I would as well,' said Francesca, 'only I hate vegetables. But it isn't very kind to kill things, is it?'

'That's all very well for you children,' said Filomena. 'You aren't vampires, like your Auntie Varvara. It's not

6

natural for vampires, that's all I'm saying.'

'Why aren't the rest of us vampires?' Marco asked. 'I've never understood.'

'You just aren't, that's all,' said Filomena. 'Vampires are very rare. As rare as musical geniuses. Perhaps rarer. Only one born in every few million children. Still, you shouldn't grumble. You've all of you got your special characteristics. Pass the marmalade, dear, will you?'

Special characteristics, yes, indeed. The whole family is endowed with special gifts. Some of these are more useful than others. Some (like Auntie Varvara being a vampire, even though she's turned vegetarian on account of her soft heart) could be called disabilities, but even Auntie Varvara can move things about the place just by thinking about it. My talents you already know about, and everyone else's gifts will be revealed in the fullness of time.

But the moment has come to write the words that every Narrator loves, a kind of 'Open Sesame' for stories, those magic words that signal the beginning. Here they are ...

Chapter 1
58, Azalea Avenue

The small van belonging to the Fantora family will shortly be taking us to our new home.

'Other people,' said Rosie, 'have a pantechnicon, and neighbours commenting on the furniture as it goes in and out.'

'We haven't got any furniture, dear,' said Eddie, 'so we'll just put all our things in the van. We ought to get to Azalea Avenue early, before all the new stuff starts arriving from the shops.'

So, as everyone is getting ready, I think there is time to tell you a little about the new house. It's not quite what we're used to, and I can tell you there were quite a number of complaints about 58, Azalea Avenue before the Fantoras decided to go ahead and buy it.

'That'll have to go,' said Rosie, when the family went to view the house. She was pointing to a wooden plaque hanging above the front door, with the name Sunnyvale painted on it in letters which curled about all over the place.

'I think it's rather a cheerful sort of name,' said Auntie Varvara.

'I don't want a cheerful name. I don't want any name at all. What's wrong with a number? 58 is a very pleasant kind of number.'

Eddie said, 'Turrets had a name. You never minded that.'

'Turrets had turrets. It was at least accurate.' Rosie sniffed. 'This house is set in a garden which is not a vale of any kind, and the weather in this part of the world is many things, but rarely, if ever, sunny.'

'I'll make it sunny,' said Francesca, 'and then the name will be true.'

Francesca's gift, apart from starting fires when she's extremely cross, is a very useful one. She can change the weather. She can't quite manage it over a wide area yet, but she is still very young. All I can tell you is that the sun shines in our garden every summer, and the children have always made a huge snowman at Christmas time, whether there's snow in the rest of the district or not.

Rosie sighed and went into the house. Nothing more was said about the sign, but I'm prepared to bet that it'll be gone when we drive up to the front door later on this morning.

The rooms at Azalea Avenue were disappointingly square and small. Turrets had been a Victorian building with high ceilings and plenty of ornamental glass set into the doors and windows.

'It's got double-glazing,' said Eddie, who was always one to look on the bright side. 'It'll be nice and quiet. And warm in winter. The central heating looks efficient. It was a bit rickety and wobbly at Turrets, you must admit. Remember all the noises in the pipes?'

'And look, everybody, a serving-hatch!' said Auntie Varvara, sticking her head through a little window set into the wall between the kitchen and the dining-room. 'How useful that'll be, won't it?'

'Come and see the bedrooms, children,' said Rosie. 'Where's Marco?'

'Here I am.'

'Thank goodness. I thought you'd disappeared again. Follow me.'

Rosie led the way upstairs and the children trooped obediently behind her, even Marco. He's the quiet one in the family: vague, absent-minded, elusive. He would rather lie on the floor and write a poem than do anything else at all. His gift (and a most valuable one for someone with his temperament) is invisibility. He was very young indeed when he discovered that by taking his clothes off he could disappear entirely. This used to be a bit of a problem when he was a toddler. Jugs of milk would quite suddenly leap into the air and pour their contents all over the floor, my tail would be pulled very hard by unseen hands, and once every single thing in the outside dustbin was spread out over the kitchen floor. Then Rosie had a brilliant idea. She stuck a small, round piece of plaster right in the centre of Marco's back, in the very place where he couldn't possibly reach it, and whenever he shed his clothes and vanished, the plaster could be clearly seen, floating about seemingly in thin air. It has to be said, of course, that the clever boy worked out that other people could take the plaster off for him, and Bianca became his chief ally when it came to playing tricks on the grown-ups or the other children at school.

'You girls could share this big bedroom in the front,' said Rosie, 'and Marco could have the little room next door.'

'I don't want to share,' said Francesca, beginning to pout a little. 'I like a room to myself. And Monkey and Leopard like a room to themselves. They would say so if they weren't packed in a box.'

Bianca whispered to Francesca, 'Don't worry, Francesca. We'll have lots of fun. Monkey and Leopard will love it. Honestly. All your toys can talk to all my toys and we'll have tea parties and picnics every day if you like.'

This was more than idle chit-chat on Bianca's part. What Bianca does, and has done ever since she was tiny is bring things to life. Many's the dolls' tea party I've sat in on in Bianca's room, with all the dolls and the teddy bears chatting away and moving around. Marco's toy soldiers can have battles any time they like, and thanks to Bianca, Monkey and Leopard, who used to sit and be ornaments on Francesca's chest of drawers, now talk to her and follow her around. They would go to school with her and to the shops as well, but Filomena won't allow it.

'There's no need,' she says, 'to flaunt gifts in front of people. That would be vulgar. Just as those who are rich shouldn't flaunt their wealth.'

It's not only toys that Bianca can animate, it's furniture and objects as well. She had a naughty trick, some time ago, of getting Eddie's favourite armchair to dance about and whistle snatches of the latest hits, just as he had settled down with the evening paper after a hard day at work. Rosie put a stop to that.

'Just do that to your father once more,' she said mildly, 'and I'll put something in your cornflakes that'll turn your teeth green.'

Eddie's armchair has never moved an inch from that day to this. Bianca is a sensible child. She has dark eyes that sparkle with laughter or temper, long curly dark hair tied up in a pony tail, and very long legs that enable her to run faster and climb trees better than most boys. She talks too much, is bossy, cheeky, obstinate, and completely charming. Generally, because of this quite unfair charm of hers, she gets her own way, but when she doesn't, she never makes life a misery. She's the organizer in the house. If she hadn't been at dancing class, Auntie Varvara's veggie burgers would never have set the house on fire.

When the children had walked around their bedrooms, examined their parents' bedroom, peered out of the windows (and seen rows and rows of houses looking just like their own, with square windows and long, rectangular gardens) and opened and shut all the cupboard doors, they were sent downstairs to get Filomena to look at her granny flat.

'Granny flat!' said Filomena derisively. 'What a name! And it's not a flat at all. Just a loft conversion.'

'But with two large rooms,' said Eddie. 'That *is* a feature, you must admit. The second room is exactly right for Varvara.'

'Oh yes,' said Auntie Varvara. 'I do love a sloping roof. It's so romantic. If only I'd known, I'd never have planned my holiday for this particular time ... only those tours of Dracula country do get booked up so far in advance ...'

'... and you weren't to know in January that in July you'd start a fire with your veggie burgers,' said Filomena, rather unnecessarily, I thought. 'Still, you'll

13

have a day or two after we move in to sort yourself out before you have to leave. Now let's look at this granny flat of yours, Eddie. Are there plenty of shelves for my wools?'

'I'll put up shelves when we move in,' said Eddie soothingly. 'It's a shame about your window though. All you can see is the sky.'

Filomena glanced upwards. 'About the only thing worth looking at around here, the sky is. I reckon I'm lucky to be missing most of what's going on at ground level. Anyway, you know me. It's all in the wools, isn't it? I get all the panoramas and vistas I can cope with in the wools, and that's a fact.'

Filomena was speaking no more than the truth. What she does is knit. I can hear you saying to yourselves: there's nothing at all remarkable in that – most grandmothers knit. This is quite true and yet I say again: hers is a very special gift, for where other grannies are enmeshed in bootees, bedjackets, cabled pullovers, Aran cardigans, Fair Isle mittens, and tea-cosies made out of leftovers, Filomena is transforming the threads of the past into a fabric that will form the future. This is another way of saying that she knows, from what she is knitting, what will happen in the days ahead.

'It's not an easy gift,' she often used to say. 'It requires the power to read what the wool is saying. You have to understand the patterns made by the needles. It calls for a deep knowledge of the colours ... the ability to see them for what they are, like the orange that appeared before the fire, for example. There they were, long threads of orange and red and yellow in a mainly grey background, and I thought it was a forecast of bright sunshine.' Filomena shook her head sadly. 'A most terrible lapse on my part. Still, I've said it once and I'll say it again. It's hard to change the future, even if you do know what it's going to be. Some things, of course, are inevitable, but my gift enables me to be prepared. I should have foreseen the fire ... yes, I should have foreseen it.'

Filomena expressed herself satisfied with the granny flat. She was fond of saying that she needed very little to make her happy.

'As long as I've got my wools,' she said, 'and room for my trampoline. There *is* room for my trampoline, isn't there, Eddie?'

'Not in here, I shouldn't think,' said Eddie. 'Perhaps in the dining-room.'

'Or you could put it in my room while I'm on holiday,' said Auntie Varvara, 'and then you won't have to go traipsing up and down stairs.'

'That's very kind of you, dear,' said Filomena.

I should have told you, shouldn't I, that every afternoon at four o'clock, Filomena takes off her long, mauve cardigan and her porridge-coloured skirt, winds the grey plaits falling down her back around her head, and puts on a bright purple tracksuit. Then she spends a good half-hour on the trampoline, bouncing, turning, somersaulting. 'Shaking myself up a bit' is what she calls it.

The fact that the loft was converted into a space suitable for Filomena and Auntie Varvara persuaded the Fantoras that Sunnyvale (there, I'm doing it – I'm calling it by name) was the ideal home. Eddie liked the garden, with its little greenhouse right down at the bottom, by the back hedge, and Rosie liked the kitchen with its waste-disposal unit and double stainless-steel sink. And me? Do you want to know what I thought of the place? I liked it. The whole house was carpeted in thick, soft stuff that your paws sank into most deliciously. That seemed a great advantage. Turrets had been dreadfully draughty. I had made a mental note of a corner of the patio which I calculated would catch the best of the sunshine in the afternoon. The mornings I intended to spend on Francesca's bed in the square of sunlight to which I had paid particular attention when we viewed the house for the first time.

Here I have to confess (though Narrators and Keepers

of Files are not supposed to let their personal feelings show) that I am besotted. I love Francesca. She talks to me more than any other member of the family, strokes me, makes a fuss of me, and actually likes me to sleep on her bed. It was Francesca who burst into tears when she thought I was missing after the fire. I had jumped after the fire. I had jumped into one of Filomena's knitting-baskets to hide from the flames. When I emerged, Francesca gathered me into her arms and said, 'Oh, Ozzy, you're not dead ... I'm so glad ...' and burst out crying all over again. So, I'm biased as far as she's concerned, and I admit it. I think she's a beautiful child, and there's nothing more to be said.

I can hear the van now, revving up outside the Belmont Private Hotel. Such of our possessions as survived the fire have been piled into the back of the van. It's time for us to go. Who knows what adventures await us in our new home?

EXTRACT FROM MY FILES NO. 1:

Auntie Varvara's Holiday Brochure

TRANSYLVANIAN MYSTERY TOURS, INC.

Have you ever wondered if it's true? Do VAMPIRES live in the CARPATHIAN MOUNTAINS? Is COUNT DRACULA alive and well?

Come and find out ... Join us on our MYSTERY TOUR.

7 nights at a genuine TRANSYLVANIAN inn for ONLY £189 inclusive. Try our traditional Transylvanian soft drink Dra-cola!

Follow the VAMPIRE trail. Conducted Tours of DRACULA'S CASTLE and surrounding woods.

DO YOU DARE TO BE ONE OF US?

FILL IN THE COUPON BELOW:

Name ....

Address ....

I/We wish to join the Mystery Tour starting on 12th September, I enclose the deposit of £50.

Signature .... Date ....

AND LOOK FORWARD TO THE HOLIDAY OF A LIFETIME!

U Schrimior-Edoff

Managing Director

TMT Inc

Chapter 2
Moving in

Have you ever moved in to a new house? If you have, you do not need to be reminded of how exhausting it is. If you have not, and can avoid doing so, I would strongly recommend that course of action. Of course, cats in general – and myself in particular – have a very hearty dislike of disturbances in their routines, and if ever anything shook a body around and never gave it a minute's rest, it's moving house.

Still, now we are settled, I can tell you about the whole experience in a more organized way. The first thing that I noticed as we drove up to our new house was that the painted sign saying Sunnyvale had indeed been removed. Everyone else was too preoccupied even to look, because there, in a long line that stretched half way down the Avenue, were about six pantechnicons all waiting to deliver our new furniture.

Eddie unlocked the front door and one by one, the huge vehicles opened and out came beds and chairs and tables and lamps, a cooker, a fridge, a freezer and a dishwasher.

'What do we want one of those for?' said Eddie. 'We've never had one before.'

'No reason not to be adventurous. A new start in a new house,' Rosie smiled sweetly back.

Chests of drawers, cupboards, sofas and armchairs followed, then a TV set, a piano and a home computer.

Rosie stood in the hall and told the men from each van exactly where everything was supposed to go.

'Bunk beds in the left-hand front room,' she'd say, or, 'Small brown cupboard in the right-hand back.'

Then the men would trip up the stairs with enormous loads on their backs, just as though they were dealing with the contents of a doll's house. Perhaps it was something Rosie had put in the tea. We'd brought flasks full of tea from the Belmont, and had given some to the drivers. It's my belief that Rosie had added something to it. Oh, nothing dangerous, just one of her magic herbs, whose properties included the giving of strength and energy to men who had to move lots of furniture about. Because, you see, Rosie is a cook. I don't mean meals, although of course she does meals as well, just like any other parent. No, Rosie concocts and otherwise puts together potions. For anything anybody wants. There are potions to make your hair grow, to make your hair curl, to make your hair shine, to make you thinner, or fatter, to whiten your teeth, banish bad breath, eliminate pimples or eradicate freckles, cure stomach-ache, toothache, headache, to put you to sleep and to wake you up. There's a potion for everything you can think of, and for a few things which would never occur to you. There's certainly one to give you strength and energy. Rosie gives it to Eddie on a Monday morning. There's even, for instance, a potion to make you invisible, but this Rosie will only use in an emergency because, she says, it has toxic side effects which she hasn't yet managed to iron out of the formula. Rosie's other gift (a frightfully useful one, I always think) is being able to fly, all by herself and without using a broomstick or any other mechanical device. When Rosie says, 'I'm just flying down to the shops for a dozen eggs', she means it literally. She has to be careful and not let too many people see her, but that's quite easy. Most grown-ups are preoccupied with this and that and never look around at all, and the children who have seen her and said to their parents, 'Look, there's a lady flying along up in the sky!' are told not to be daft, and sometimes even told off for telling fibs.

Once the furniture was in, the fun began. Auntie Varvara was most useful, of course, being able to move things around simply by thinking about it. She took up a central position in the hall and dealt with every problem as it came along. She never complained when people changed their minds. All it took was a shake of her head and, hey presto, chairs and tables sailed through the air and landed as softly as feathers in the right place.

'No, move the sofa onto that wall ... I don't like that picture there, try it over the fireplace ... Has anyone seen my wool basket? The one with all the browns in it ... where's Marco? ... I don't want the top bunk, so there ... is this the right time to start the train-set going, honestly ... Come and put a plug on this or we'll never get any supper ... No, Varvara, I have not seen your brochures ... Has anyone seen Marco? ... Give this cup of coffee to your father ... What do you mean, Bianca's being unfair? ... Take Leopard off the dishdrainer, please ... Where did you put the curtain hooks? ... What do you mean it won't fit? ... Is Marco in his room? ...'

It all became too much for me, so I crept out of the house, hoping to find a bit of peace and quiet in the garden.

Eddie was there, talking over the fence to a pleasant-looking lady dressed in a flowered overall. She was saying, 'I said to Arnold it was you! I said, it's that Mr Fantora from Fantora's Greengrocery and Florist's Shop. What a coincidence! I've passed it ever so often.'

'I hope you will come in one day ...'

'Ooh, I will. Now we're neighbours.'

'We've got everything you could possibly want.'

'It does sound lovely. I'll come in next time, I promise, only usually, you see, I get everything all in one fell swoop, as it were, at the supermarket.'

'But not as fresh as in my shop,' said Eddie. 'You see, I grow almost everything myself. Coconuts, avocados, orchids, asparagus, asparagus ferns, fennel, aubergines, yams, breadfruit, kumquats, kiwi fruit … the list is endless.'

'Fancy!' said the lady, visibly amazed. 'I didn't think you could grow half those things up here. Whatever will they think of next?'

'Anything you'd like, Mrs … ?'

'Collins. Dora Collins.'

'Mrs Collins … anything you'd like, just you tell me, and I'll grow it for you.'

'Well, thank you very much. And if you need anything, any help at all, moving in and that, just you give me a shout.'

'I will. Many thanks.'

Dora Collins hurried into her own house. Eddie walked down the garden and into the greenhouse. I followed him. I like Eddie. He's a quiet, unassuming sort of person, and a bit of a disappointment to his mother. I think she fancied the idea of her only son being something really spectacular – a wizard, perhaps, swishing about in a purple robe encrusted with stars. It's true, her daughter is a vampire, but can you count her, since she became a vegetarian? Filomena is doubtful. Eddie has magic powers, of course he has, and it's true to say that the amassing of the Fantora family fortune, such as it is, is largely due to him. Still, although he's gifted in certain directions, he lacks (so his mother and sister say) ambition. But this is his gift: he can make anything grow anywhere. Palm trees in the bath, water-lilies on top of the kitchen cupboard, grapevines on the bookshelves, daffodils in the ironing baskets; anything you'd like, anywhere you please.

Therefore the Fantora Greengrocery and Florist's Shop on Buckley Parade (known locally as the FGF) flourishes, as you can imagine. No need to go racing up to town for exotic fruits or unusual flowers, they're right here on the edge of the Barton Bridge Estate. The motto over the door of the shop is 'I can get it for you'. Before the fire, Turrets was full of small pots in which Eddie was nurturing his special orders: a pineapple for Mrs Withers, or a small lemon tree hung with lemons for PC Wright. Not only can Eddie grow anything, he can also talk to his plants. The rest of the family think him rather eccentric in this matter, but Eddie insists that his plants all chat to him and he most certainly chats right back. Many's the time I've caught him laughing with a lettuce, passing the time of day with a potato, or deep in conversation with a cauliflower. Sometimes I can half-hear their replies, but I never know whether I've really heard them, or whether it's my overactive imagination. The family takes these gifts for granted, as is often the case with families. They don't think there's anything at all exciting about making things grow. The children would have preferred their father to be a bus driver or a fighter pilot or a newsreader on the television. The adults all think Eddie could be more forceful, and yet he has a dream. I know about it because he tells me everything and I listen. It's not a secret, so I can tell you. The only reason no one else knows about it is because they're not interested.

'Never mind, Ozzy,' he says to me sometimes, 'they'll sit up and take notice when I've got it right.'

Got what right? Why, the Fruit Salad Tree. A tree on which you will find growing, all at the same time, apples, oranges, pears, apricots, bananas, grapes, and pineapples. Wouldn't that be tremendous? Eddie's voice trembles with emotion as he describes it to me.

'You could have variations, Ozzy. You could choose

whatever combination of fruit you wanted. Strawberries, watermelons, and peaches. Some trees could have nuts included. Think how famous I'll be when I've perfected it ...' And he'd go off into a daydream. All his experiments to date have been unsuccessful. Filomena would probably say that he was flying in the face of Nature, just as Auntie Varvara was by changing the eating habits of a lifetime, but Eddie is convinced that his day will come, and maybe it will. Eddie obviously thought that the greenhouse might do the trick.

'The light is right here, Ozzy, do you see?' he said. 'I'll start experimenting as soon as I can. Not today, of course ... in fact, I suppose I'd better go back to the house and help hang curtains and things ... Still, I'll get down to it as soon as I've got this lot settled in nicely.'

'This lot' was all the plants he had managed to rescue from the window sills of Turrets: a few cacti and succulents, a jade plant or two, and a couple of aloes.

'We'll soon add to them, Ozzy, don't worry. We'll get all sorts, and not just for the greenhouse. Camellias, azaleas, gardenias, lobelias, forsythias, japonicas ... all sorts. I fancy a magnolia, right in the middle of the lawn ... and tomatoes ... and strawberries. Oh, it'll be splendid. Won't it, everyone?' He smiled and nodded at the inhabitants of the few pots on the greenhouse shelves, but I couldn't catch their answer.

'You should,' I said to him, 'have dug up all the plants from the garden of Turrets. That would have saved you a lot of trouble.'

'That, Ozzy, would have been vandalism, you naughty old thing. But,' he grinned, 'look what I've got in this carrier bag.'

I looked and it seemed to me that all he had there were bits of twig and leaf and assorted branches. I told him so.

'Cuttings, Ozzy. That's what these are.' He started taking the bits and pieces out of the bag and laid them side by side on the shelf. 'I went back and snipped a little from all my favourites. Now we'll have what we want, and the owners of whatever it is that gets built where Turrets used to be will still have a wonderful garden. The best of both worlds, Ozzy, the best of both worlds.'

When I went back into the house, driven by hunger, things were quieter. Bianca and Francesca were in their room. Bianca had animated the inhabitants of the dolls' house, which was one of the few things saved from the fire. It seemed to be moving day for the dolls as well, only Bianca had seen to it that in this miniature world, everything went according to the plans of the children.

'Sandy,' said Bianca to one of the girl dolls, 'this can be your room.'

'I want velvet curtains and a silk counterpane,' said Sandy, who was rather spoilt.

'These *are* velvet curtains,' said Bianca.

'No, they're not. They're cotton. They used to be a nightdress once. I remember.' Sandy frowned.

'Then use your imagination,' said Bianca. 'I know that's a knitted blanket, but it can be a silk counterpane if you imagine it hard enough.'

'Why can't you turn things into other things, that's what I want to know.'

'I can't, that's all,' Bianca said. 'You ought to be satisfied with what I *can* do. If you don't shut up and move into your new house properly, I'll make you all stiff and silent again, so there!'

Sandy kept quiet, and helped her friend Candy to rearrange the furniture in the dolls' house so as to make it seem like a new home altogether. I sat on Francesca's bed and listened to the voices: human voices, and higher, thinner dolls' voices. I heard Monkey and Leopard deciding on the best place to sleep in lower, growly animal voices. I think I must have dozed off for a while, because when I woke up, the sky outside was striped with evening colours – lilac and pink and apricot. Doors were banging. That was what woke me up. Shouts of 'Marco' echoed round the house. I went downstairs. Rosie was cross.

'How dare he disappear just today when everybody's so busy?'

'He isn't in his room,' said Eddie, 'unless he's taken his plaster off.'

'Bianca?' Rosie frowned at her elder daughter.

'Don't look at me,' said Bianca. 'I haven't seen him all afternoon. And I have not touched his plaster.'

'Francesca?'

'I've been with Bianca all the time.'

'He'll turn up,' said Filomena. She was knitting something cream-coloured with lots of bumps and bobbles and cables and twisted stitches. I've become quite an interpreter of her work over the years and I can tell you that the colour cream stands for new beginnings, and all the twists and bobbles mean that the day has been difficult, set about with problems and little arguments no larger than a piece of grit in a shoe, but just as annoying.

'I feel,' said Filomena, 'a stretch of stocking stitch coming on. Everything is smoothing down, flattening out nicely. It would never do that if Marco were in any kind of trouble. He'll turn up.'

'Has someone been calling me?' said Marco, putting his head round the door.

'Yes, you wicked child,' said Rosie. 'Where have you been? We've looked everywhere for you.'

'I've been in the bath,' said Marco.

'I looked in there,' said Eddie. 'The bath had no water in it. The whole place was empty.'

'No, it wasn't,' said Marco. 'I was in it. Only you couldn't see me.'

'What were you doing,' said Filomena, 'if you weren't bathing?'

'I was writing a poem.'

'But why the bathroom?' said Eddie. 'Not to mention why the bath?'

'It's easily the best place to be when there's moving going on. No one comes in and out with bits of furniture. There's nothing to arrange in a bathroom once the towels and toothbrushes are out. And it's quite comfy lying in the bath. Even without water. I've had a very quiet day. Is supper ready?'

Everyone laughed and went in to supper. So just remember, when your family moves house, make for the bathroom.

EXTRACT FROM MY FILES NO. 2:
Marco's Poem

Moving in by Marco Fantora
Today my family moved in to number 58.
We started moving early.
We finished moving late.

Everybody's got a room.
Mine is small and square.
I've got a cupboard where I've put everything I wear.

My books are on the shelves,
My soldiers in their box.
I've folded my pyjamas and rolled up all my socks.

They can't say I've done nothing
I've put everthing away,
But I like it in this bathtub
So I'll stay in it all day.

Chapter 3
Otter Street Primary School

Filomena's cream-coloured wool was telling no more than the truth. It was a time of new beginnings for all of us, but especially for Bianca and Marco who had to start in an entirely new school shortly after we moved to Azalea Avenue. It was called Otter Street Primary. Rosie took them to the gates on the first day.

'I don't see why we couldn't have stayed on at our old school,' said Bianca. 'Francesca has. She gets a lift with Eddie in the van every day. It's not fair.'

'Only because Otter Street hasn't any vacancies till January in Francesca's class. Otter Street is much nearer as well. That's the main reason. Now, Marco, I don't want you disappearing at school. Teachers get panicky over their registers, do you understand?'

'Yes, all right,' said Marco, sighing.

'And Bianca, please see that he eats his sandwiches.'

Rosie kissed them goodbye. 'I must fly. There's still Auntie Varvara's muesli to make ...' And she sailed away, up and up and over the trees. Only one little girl saw her (everyone else was busy in the playground) and she pulled at her mother's skirt and said, 'Mum, I want to go home, I think I'm ill. I've just seen a lady flying over those houses.'

'Honestly, Sheila,' said her mother, 'I've heard some good excuses in my time, but that takes the biscuit, it does really ... Now you get in to school and don't let me hear such nonsense again!'

I knew something was wrong the minute Bianca and Marco came home, that first afternoon. They hardly said a word to anyone, just slid along to Marco's room as soon as they'd had a biscuit and a drink. I followed them, of course, and curled up on Marco's bed and pretended to be asleep. A Narrator has to be constantly alert for problems and conflicts and interesting situations, and if Marco's red-rimmed eyes were anything to go by, something not very pleasant had been going on at school, and it was something I had to find out about in the interests of the Files.

'You should tell me about it, Marco,' Bianca said. 'You shouldn't just keep it to yourself.'

'I don't see what you can do about it. You're in another class. I was going to disappear, but I practically promised Rosie I wouldn't.'

'And anyway,' said Bianca, 'disappearing's not going to help, at least not disappearing in the way you mean.

33

So, who are these bullies and what did they do?'

'They're called Malcolm Scrimsby and Jeremy Blackett. They think they're dead clever. Everyone else in the class seems to think they're dead clever too. They egg them on, encourage them. They giggled about my name at first. Then they said I must be a girl, I was so small, and how come I was so pale after such a hot summer. Jeremy said maybe I was an insect that lived under a stone.'

'And you said nothing? Did nothing?'

'They would've battered me.'

'It might have been pleasanter than just being got at all the time.'

'I hate fighting,' said Marco.

'I know you do, but sometimes you have to,' said Bianca.

'I thought they might get fed up with picking on me, but I don't think they will. I wouldn't mind so much, but they threw my sandwiches in the dustbin and tore up my work when I was out at the front with Mr Weedon.'

'Didn't you say anything to him? To Mr Weedon? He sounds just like a weed. Is he a weed?'

Marco thought for a moment. 'No, not really. It's just that he believes what Scrimsby and Blackett say and not what I say. I expect it's because he doesn't know me very well ... because I'm new.'

'OK,' said Bianca. 'Leave it to me. I'll sort them out

tomorrow ... and I'll get you to help me. They'll regret they ever came anywhere near you.'

'What'll we do, Bianca? Do tell me. Go on.'

'I'll tell you tomorrow,' she giggled. 'School's going to be ... well, a little unusual in the morning. Wait and see. I've got to write a composition for tomorrow. About my hobbies, of all the boring things.'

She left the room and I went with her. Marco would probably read till supper time. Downstairs, Rosie was preparing supper and from the dining-room came the rhythmic pinging and rubbery creaks of Filomena's trampoline. I went in search of Auntie Varvara, who was sometimes in the habit of pouring out her heart to me.

I found her in the attic room, choosing clothes suitable for a holiday in Transylvania. She was glad to see me.

'It's a problem, Ozzy,' she said. 'Will it be hot or cold? Do I need a raincoat? Or a scarf to hold my hair if the landscape is at all windswept? And should I take my new sandals? Such a problem.' She giggled. I'm not used to holidays, Ozzy. This is the first one I've ever been on without the family ... oh, Ozzy, I'm so excited ...' She sank down on to the bed, clutching a frilly blouse to her bosom.

Auntie Varvara is a romantic. She's kind and loving

and pretty in a wispy, faded sort of way, but she does have crazes which can be very troublesome. Vegetarianism is the latest, but in her time she's done macramé, modern dance, hula-hooping, roller-skating, skate-boarding, acupuncture, pottery, French, painting by numbers, do-it-yourself, and stamp collecting. Vegetarianism (which goes together with yoga classes and a fascination with the health-giving properties of one thing and another) has now lasted longer than any other craze and perhaps will last forever. Auntie Varvara is liked by us all ... well, it would be hard to dislike her ... but she's the kind of person grown-ups sigh about rather a lot whenever they're discussing her. For instance (and these are examples taken from past conversations):

'What (sigh) is going to happen to Varvara when she's old? Surely she ought to marry and have a family of her own?'

'Why (sigh) can't she stick to one job for longer than a month?'

'Why (sigh) does she believe everything she reads in books?'

And so it goes on. I think – and this is my own opinion, nothing more – that being a vampire during her formative years rather spoiled her chances of finding a husband. There can't be many teenage lads who'd be willing to risk it. Still, now that she has given up red meat and goes to yoga classes twice a week, perhaps there's hope. Especially on this holiday. If only she would dress a little more dashingly. Floral frocks with limp cardigans in pastel colours, that's Auntie Varvara's style ... sigh ... there, I'm doing it myself now!

I curled up on her bed and listened to her.

'It's going to be marvellous, Ozzy. Have you seen the brochure? Isn't it the most thrilling thing ever? Filomena has been knitting deeper and deeper shades of pink. She says it's the colour of love. I'm sure that must be for me ... wouldn't that be wonderful? I've bought this perfume. Have a sniff, Ozzy. I couldn't resist the name. It's called Fatal Kiss. Don't you think that's romantic? Have a sniff.'

'It's very nice,' I said. 'I'm sure it'll suit you very well.' I have learned over the years that white lies can sometimes give people a great deal of pleasure, and so I often tell them, as a friend and a cat. As a Narrator, however, I am bound to tell the truth, and the truth is that Auntie Varvara's perfume smelt like a cross between fly spray and burnt sugar. So dreadful was it that I was forced to make some excuse and leave the room. I muttered something about having a word with Filomena now that her trampolining was over, and fled. Filomena was sorting the colours. She did it every

evening. She knitted all through the night. I don't
know when she slept.

'Old people need very little sleep, Ozzy,' she would
say. 'Unlike cats.'

I watched her at her work. All round the room
were the wool baskets. In each basket were dozens
and dozens of different shades of the same colour, and
every colour meant something different.

'It's a mysterious process,' Filomena would say.
'It takes many years to perfect the knowledge of the
colours. Everything is in the variations. A colour means
one thing when pale, and another when dark. Colours
can be mixed, or streaked. Oh, there are no limits to
what they can tell you.'

Long ago, I used to ask her questions. How do you
know what colours to choose? And where does all the
wool come from?

'The colours pick themselves,' she would answer.
'I suppose I decide, really, but they seem to come to me
by themselves. They seem to speak to me and tell me:
"take me now, choose me to be in the fabric" and at the
end of the night, when the fabric is completed for the
next day, then I look at it and I can tell. I can tell almost
exactly what will happen. And the wool? You ask where
I get the wool, and I'll tell you. I find it, I buy it, I am

given it by everyone because everyone knows I collect it. I seek it out in jumble sales and department stores, I unpick old jerseys from the charity shop ... oh, my wool comes from far and near. I order it from woollen mills and hand-weavers. It comes from every country in the world. And once I have it, I never lose it. It gets knotted into the fabric, and the fabric of each day is made from bits and pieces of days that have gone before, days that have disappeared into the past. When I was very young, I used to think: wouldn't it be wonderful if life were like a piece of knitting? Then you could go back and undo the bits you didn't like, correct your mistakes, knit your life up again into a better pattern ... how lovely it would be to pull a thread and unravel time, unpick all the days when you were unhappy, and knit them up again into better days. Well, I discovered that you can almost do that. Not quite, but almost. The colours that come to my hand, the stitches that come into my head and ask to be knitted I seem to be unable to control, but I have learned to read the fabric. It's a bit like weather forecasting. I get it right most of the time, but I do make mistakes. Like the fire.'

Now, Filomena said, 'Hello, Ozzy,' and sighed heartily. 'I don't like the look of tonight's colours at all. An awful lot of mauve about ... the colour of bruises.'

'That'll be Marco,' I said. 'He's being bullied at school. I heard him talking to Bianca. She's got some plan for tomorrow. I don't know what it is.'

'That'll be the black, then. It often means revenge … and there's a moderately angry-looking red here and there, as well. And I suppose all this pink I'm getting must be Varvara. It's a very fluttery, hopeful sort of pink and look at this, very pale sky blue … well, that must be Varvara's flight, I expect. Poor little Marco! What a horrid mauve it is.' She sighed and looked at the clock. 'Come on, Ozzy,' she said. 'It's time to go down to supper.'

At supper, Bianca said, quite out of the blue, 'They're looking for someone at school to do crafts with Junior Four. Just one morning a week. It's because one of the mothers who goes in to do it is having a baby.'

Rosie said, 'I hope you didn't say I'd do it, did you?'

'No,' said Bianca. 'I told them my grandmother was an ace knitter and I'd ask her if she'd do it.' Bianca helped herself to more mashed potatoes.

'Me?' said Filomena. 'Teach in a school?'

'Go on, Filomena,' said Marco. 'You'd be brilliant. It'd be great having you there.'

Filomena was silent. I could tell she was remembering the mauve strands in the fabric. 'Very well,' she said at last. 'I'll go and see the Head about it. Fancy me becoming a teacher at my time of life.' She chuckled. 'I will have all the children knitting Dream Cushions.'

'What are Dream Cushions?' asked Francesca.

'You will find out what they are on your birthday ... that's not long to wait. Yes, they'll all be knitting, the boys as well.'

'Rather you than me,' said Eddie. 'All those kids – you wouldn't catch me at it.'

'But you will organize the Plant Stall for the Christmas Gala, won't you?' Bianca said. 'I said I'd ask if you would. Oh, please do. Go on. It'll be ever such fun.'

Eddie sighed. 'Bianca! The Plant Stall, is it? Oh, well, I don't see why not. I always did it at the last school.'

'That's what I said,' said Marco. 'I said you wouldn't mind. And I said that at our last school Rosie did the Cake Stall, with Auntie Varvara to help her ...'

'... and you volunteered us for that, did you?' Rosie asked. 'I might have known. You're not in the school five minutes and already the whole family's running the Christmas Gala.'

'I'm not,' said Filomena. 'I'm a part-time teacher.'

Francesca looked up from her apple crumble and smiled at her grandmother. 'Bianca says that they're going to ask you to be a fortune-teller in a proper fortune-teller's caravan with a gypsy costume on at the Christmas Gala. Don't kick me, Bianca, I *did* hear you say that.'

Marco blushed. 'We were going to ask you later, Filomena. We thought we might have to persuade you a bit.'

'Persuade me?' Filomena smiled. 'You must be joking. You try and keep me away. I'll give them fortune-telling like they've never seen before. Pass the custard, Varvara dear. What fun we shall all have!'

She seemed for the moment to have forgotten the mauve of Marco's bruises and the black that stood for revenge.

EXTRACT FROM MY FILES NO. 3:

Bianca's Composition

<u>Hobbies by Bianca Fantora</u>

My hobby is talking to my toys. My best toys are two dolls called Sandy and Candy. They have a baby called Mandy and their dog is called Shandy. My little sister has two pets called Monkey and Leopard. They are quite naughty. Leopard is very greedy and my mum has to cover up all the meat in the kitchen in case Leopard eats it. My brother likes soldiers. They have battles on the floor of his room. He writes poems and has a train set which works. My auntie does yoga, my granny likes knitting and my dad likes to do gardening. He works in a greengrocer's shop. My mum helps him in the shop sometimes. She also cooks all sorts of things. Once she made some hand lotion which smelled lovely. We have a cat called Ozzy. His hobby is sleeping.

EXTRACT FROM MY FILES NO. 4:

Filomena's Colour Chart.

Remember that all the colours can mean many different things, depending on the combinations in which they are found. This is because life is never only one thing at a time.

RED	When dark, it means anger, violence, blood. When lighter it means annoyance and minor irritations.
YELLOW	Means happiness, wealth and sunshine.
APRICOT/ PEACH	Means comfort, luxury and good food.
ORANGE	Means very hot weather, but also fire.
GREEN	Means either: new life and growth (PALE GREEN) or: illness and bad luck (LIME GREEN) or: jealousy (EMERALD GREEN) A certain shade of BLUEY-GREEN means weddings.

BLUE	Means: unhappiness (DEEP ROYAL BLUE)
	or: peace (GREENY-BLUE)
	or: anger (PURPLY-BLUE)
	or: travel (PALE BLUE)
	or: sleep (NAVY BLUE)
	or: water (GREY-BLUE)
BLACK	Means revenge, blindness, night-time. Mixed with white it means bad weather.
GREY/ BEIGE	Are the colours of ordinary life and change their meaning as bits of other colours are added to them.
PINK	Means affection, DEEP PINK means love, and if blue is added to pink to make MAUVE it means unhappy love.
PURPLE/ DEEEP MAUVE	Means pain. Intensity varies from the MAUVE of bruises to the DEEP PURPLE of very severe pain.
BROWN	Is the colour of Earth.
GOLD	Is the colour of friendship.
SILVER	Is the colour of air and the imagination.
WHITE	Is the colour of death.

Chapter 4
Revenge!

The day planned for revenge did not start well as far as Marco was concerned. Not only did he have to pack his schoolbag, eat his breakfast, collect his sandwiches, and leave the house with Bianca at what he considered to be breakneck speed, but on this particular morning a special goodbye had to be said to Auntie Varvara, who was setting forth at lunch time for the Holiday of a Lifetime. Now most people just kiss you briefly, say 'Have a good time while I'm gone' or 'I'll send you a postcard' or simply 'Cheerio', but not Auntie Varvara. For her, farewells were an opportunity for clasping her loved ones to her bosom, bestowing kisses like confetti on the tops of their heads, and even occasionally sniffing into a lace-edged hankie. Marco wondered as he went through all this whether it wouldn't be a great relief to get to school and be bullied in earnest, but all he said was, 'Have a good time, Auntie Varvara. See you soon.'

'Yes, see you soon,' said Bianca (who had had her turn and was waiting by the door). 'Write lots of postcards. Come on, Marco. Let's get a move on.'

Up Azalea Avenue they went together, with Auntie

Varvara waving at their backs until they were out of sight.

Malcolm and Jeremy were waiting as Bianca and Marco came through the school gate. They hardly noticed Bianca, because she was a girl and therefore unworthy of their attention. Instead they concentrated on Marco, and decided to limber up for the day's tortures by picking on (of all things) his satchel.

'That's a funny-looking school bag, Fantora,' said Malcolm.

'Naff,' said Jeremy. 'That's what I call it.'

'What do you call it, then, Fantora, eh? Let's have a look.' Malcolm lunged forward and snatched the satchel out of Marco's hand. He started running away down the playground with it, shouting, 'Aren't you coming to get your grotty old bag, then? Aren't you going to stop us?'

Marco just stood there quietly. All the other children, sensing that something dramatic was going on, formed a ring round Marco, shouting, 'Go on, Marco, get them! Go on, Fantora!'

'We're going to see what's in here, aren't we, Jeremy?' said Malcolm from the far end of the playground. And then they made the mistake of opening Marco's bag, and the even worse mistake of unzipping his pencil case. No one at all had been looking at Bianca while all this was going on. She had managed to place herself quite near Malcolm and Jeremy's end of the playground, near enough to do what she had to do. No sooner had the bullies opened the satchel and unzipped the pencil case than everything sprang to life at once. Felt-tip pens turned themselves into brightly-coloured little spears and hummed through the air, stabbing Malcolm and Jeremy in the shins, on the hands, in the back and the stomach. What with all the activity, a couple of their tops fell off, and soon Malcolm and Jeremy were covered in orange spots, and blue lines and yellow and green blotches where the pens had struck them.

'Cut it out!'

'Stop it!'

'What's happening?'

'Get off ...'

Their shouts rang forth over the playground as all the children clustered around Marco and gazed, speechless, at what was happening. Bianca had not quite finished, however. She turned her attention next to the contents of Malcolm and Jeremy's own bags. Slowly, all by themselves, the buckles unbuckled, and from the depths of each bag came exercise books and text books, pens and pencils, and rubbers and rulers, and like a flock of doves being released from a basket, books fluttered their leaves high over the playground. Wherever you looked, small items of stationery were hovering in the air. It was at this moment, just as Bianca had seen to it that all the contents of Marco's bag had replaced themselves neatly, just as Malcolm and Jeremy were rushing round the playground trying to clutch and claw at their belongings which were still floating about just out of reach, that Mrs Harpenden, the Deputy Head, came out to blow the whistle for Morning Assembly.

'What,' she thundered, 'is the meaning of this?'

Malcolm and Jeremy looked up, and even as she spoke, all their possessions fell to earth and landed in an unspeakable mess at their feet.

'Whose things,' Mrs Harpenden continued without the smallest pause, 'are these?'

'Mine, please, Miss,' said Malcolm.

'Mine, please, Miss,' said Jeremy.

'Very well,' said Mrs Harpenden. 'What I have to do is quite clear. As you are both obviously training to become refuse collectors, I shall help you as much as I possibly can. You are to go to every classroom and take their waste-paper baskets one by one to the big dustbins at the back of the school. Empty each basket and take it back to where it belongs. You will, I think, have somewhat different views on litter by the end of the morning.'

Mrs Harpenden smiled at Malcolm and Jeremy. She continued, 'I see too that the playground, even though

49

it is the beginning of term is, nevertheless, satisfyingly full of crisp packets and autumn leaves. I shall expect you to collect them all before you embark upon your indoor tidying activities. The rest of you, lead in to Morning Assembly, please.'

Bianca winked at Marco as they went in. Their revenge had begun.

Meanwhile, back at 58, Azalea Avenue, Auntie Varvara was fluttering around her luggage, checking that she had everything before the taxi came to take her to the airport.

'Passport … traveller's cheques … ticket … sandwiches … where are the sandwiches?'

'Here they are, dear,' said Rosie, coming out of the kitchen with a large Tupperware box in her hand. 'Just what you asked for – cream cheese, beansprouts, and chopped herbs, and sesame seed and carrot pâté. It's a waste really, isn't it, you not eating all the food they're going to give you on the aeroplane.'

Auntie Varvara wrinkled her nose. 'Synthetic,' she said, 'that's what that is. Plastic food … no knowing the artificial colours and preservatives that go into aeroplane food.'

'But what about Transylvania?' said Rosie. 'I won't be there to make you whatever you fancy.'

Auntie Varvara's face lit up. 'There, I'm sure, we shall

have real country food, potatoes and pulses and swedes and turnips galore. Oh, I'm so excited! Filomena, what does the fabric say? Are the omens good?'

Filomena took out the knitting which she'd rolled up and put into a basket by the door. She spread it out over her lap and nodded. 'Lots of pale blue ... that's the air travel, and pink. Well, that's romance, as you know. That's exciting, isn't it? I wonder who ...
And this nice rich brown could be ... well, almost anything really – a wooden building perhaps, or even a dark stranger. The mauve of bruises is fading a little, Marco's feeling better, I expect. Well, Varvara, all's well, I think.'

Auntie Varvara sighed. 'Oh, dear, the taxi will soon be here. I'd better check through everything again. I wouldn't like to forget anything. Passport ... tickets ... traveller's cheques ... sandwiches ...'

And with that I closed my eyes and transported myself, as all Narrators are able to do at will, to Otter Street Primary School.

* * *

Malcolm and Jeremy, as well as being bullies, were not that clever. They could not quite understand what had happened in the playground that morning ... it had been weird, all right. On that they were agreed, but neither of them connected the weirdness with Marco in any way. Marco explained this to Bianca during the dinner hour.

'That's OK,' said Bianca, 'they will. Eventually. But,' she added, 'we're going to have a bit more fun with them first. What've you got this afternoon?'

'Art,' said Marco. 'They'll manage to spill my paints all over my work, I expect.'

'Anything they can do, I can do better. You should know that by now. See you.' Bianca ran off to play with her new friends.

'How are you going – ' Marco began to say, but she had gone. He wondered how Bianca was going to manage anything from her classroom, which was right at the other end of the corridor from his. He shouldn't have worried. The art lesson had only been going for about ten minutes (and Malcolm and Jeremy were only just warming up for action with the odd flick of paint on to Marco's work from time to time), when there was a knock at the door.

'Come,' shouted Mr Weedon and in walked Bianca. She smiled sweetly.

'Please, sir, Mrs Dawes says would you give these

envelopes to your children to take home? It's a collection for the blind.'

'Yes, of course, dear,' said Mr Weedon. 'Just go and put them over there.'

Bianca went. As she leaned forward to put the envelopes down on the desk, two things happened. First, the jam jars into which Malcolm and Jeremy had been dipping their brushes sailed into the air, hung for a moment, one above Malcolm's head, the other above Jeremy's, then slowly and carefully tipped themselves up and emptied their murky contents all over the two boys' heads. Streams of blacky-greeny-purply liquid gushed over their faces and ran in small rivulets down their necks, soaking finally into their pullovers and shirts and vests. Their shrieks of horror distracted Mr Weedon from the fact that their two paintbrushes had jumped up from the desk and were having a very jolly time, painting orange squiggles on Mr Weedon's brown leatherette jacket, which was hanging on the back of his chair. The class could only look on, astonished and bewildered by what was happening. After a few happy moments watching this chaos, Bianca restored everything to normal and said, 'Thank you very much, sir,' and left the room.

When Mr Weedon had calmed down, he asked the class to tell him what had happened.

'Please, sir, the jam jars just got up and spilt themselves.'

'All over Scrimsby and Blackett.'

'Honest. They did. All by themselves.'

'And the brushes. Scrimsby 'n' Blackett's brushes ...'

'I suppose,' Mr Weedon smiled thinly, 'you're going to tell me the brushes painted squiggles all over my coat by themselves too?'

'Yes.'

'Yes, they did.'

Thirty heads nodded in agreement.

'Well,' said Mr Weedon, rising somewhat shakily to his feet, 'you may all have taken leave of your senses, but I still retain a few of mine and they tell me this: if Scrimsby and Blackett's brushes make a pop art masterpiece of my coat, then Scrimsby and Blackett are responsible. If, moreover, not one but *two* jam jars of disgusting paint-water are spilt, then I must assume that they were spilt by the boys whose jam jars they are.' He glared at Malcolm and Jeremy. 'Therefore, and bearing in mind that the two of you are so keen on painting, I shall keep both of you behind tomorrow night. The bicycle shed at the front of the school is in dire need of a coat of paint. Kindly inform your parents of this punishment and be ready for some rather more strenuous painting tomorrow afternoon than you have had today. You may also kiss your afternoon playtime goodbye. You will be much too busy sponging down my coat for any such frivolities.'

Bianca and Marco spent the whole of afternoon play giggling and whispering together. Soon, soon their revenge would be complete, and Malcolm and Jeremy would never bother Marco again.

At 3.20 p.m. exactly, five minutes before home-time, there was a knock on the door of Mr Weedon's classroom. This day, only the second day of a new school year, had nearly been too much for Mr Weedon. An image of the days between today and Christmas filled his mind: an endlessly unrolling ribbon of horrors such as he had had to deal with during Art. Therefore, it was in a weary voice that he croaked out, 'Come!'

Bianca came in, smiling even more sweetly than she had before. 'Please, sir, will you excuse Marco Fantora? He's my brother and we have a dentist's appointment.'

'Take him. Take him.' Mr Weedon waved his hand, thinking: *I wish you'd take the whole class while you're at it.*

Marco, who had been expecting Bianca, followed her out of the room.

By the time the bell rang for the end of the school day, Marco's clothes and belongings were in a carrier bag being taken home by Bianca. Marco himself was invisible. He was waiting beside the school gate, ready for what he had to do.

Malcolm and Jeremy had just come out of Murray's sweetshop and were looking forward to their cola cubes.

'Here,' Malcolm held out the bag.

'Don't mind if I do,' said a voice, and the bag was snatched out of Malcolm's hand and danced along all by itself, about three feet above the pavement.

'Come back! Come back here! Those are our cola cubes.'

'There will be no more cola cubes,' intoned a voice. It was Marco's voice, but sounded much deeper when he spoke through his cupped hands. It was a technique he had been perfecting for ages.

'Who is it?' said Malcolm. 'Is it you, Jeremy?'

'Don't be daft,' said Jeremy. 'Of course it isn't me. It's someone hiding. Playing a trick.'

'No trick,' wailed Marco. 'This is the Revenge of the Fantoras.'

'If it's that pipsqueak Marco, I'll batter him,' said Malcolm.

'Give over,' said Jeremy. 'As if he'd have the nerve. Little tiddler like him.'

'The Revenge of the Fantoras,' Marco growled,

unperturbed. 'If so much as one hair is touched on the head of a member of the Fantora family, do you know what will happen?'

'No, what, surprise me!' spluttered Jeremy, who was nevertheless beginning to turn a little pale.

Marco came up to him and grabbed him by the tie.

'Hey, leave that out! I'm choking ... what are you trying to do? Strangle me?'

'Exactly,' breathed Marco's disembodied voice in what he hoped was a ghastly whisper. He needed one of his hands for grabbing the tie and yanking it firmly upwards.

'Oh, oh, I've had enough. Stop! Leave me alone!' Jeremy sounded close to tears.

'And you will leave Marco Fantora alone?'

'Yes, yes, I promise you ... whoever you are.'

'What about your friend?' Marco whispered, yanking with his other hand at Malcolm's tie. Malcolm had been rooted to the spot with his mouth open and his eyes wide for the last couple of minutes.

'Yes, I promise too,' burbled Malcolm.

'Excellent.' Marco dropped the ties and put his hands over his mouth again. 'Do not forget. I will be watching your every move. Day and night, winter and summer.'

'But who *are* you?' spluttered Malcolm, who felt a

bit braver now he wasn't being choked by his tie.

'I,' boomed Marco, 'am the Scarlet Eye of Vengeance. I am everywhere.' He launched into a laugh so hideous that it even impressed Bianca, who had been watching all this from the other side of the road.

'Go now,' Marco said, 'and remember, I am watching you. The ever-watchful Scarlet Eye.'

Malcolm and Jeremy ran down the road, not even stopping to pick up their bag of cola cubes.

Bianca crossed the road and picked up the sweets.

'Great!' she said to Marco, popping one into her mouth. 'You were terrific. Where did you get that Scarlet Eye stuff? That was dead good.'

'It just came into my head,' said Marco. 'D'you think they'll try anything now?'

'I'd be surprised if they dared to come to school after the kind of day they've had today. They won't be bothering you again, though, so we don't have to worry. Here,' she thrust the carrier bag towards where she thought Marco's hands might be. 'You'd better go behind the hedge and get dressed. Quickly.'

'What happened at school today, Marco?' asked Rosie at supper-time.

'Nothing much,' said Marco. 'Is there any chocolate sauce to go with this ice cream?'

EXTRACT FROM MY FILES NO. 5:

A Postcard from Auntie Varvara

Dear Everyone,

This is a picture of our aeroplane.
Isn't it kind of them to give us free
cards to send home? Sandwiches v.
welcome. The person next to me had
beef stew in a bright orange sauce.
Yuck!! Will write from the hotel.
Love,

Varvara.

THE FANTORA FAMILY
58, AZALEA AVE.
BARTON BRIDGE ESTATE
MANCHESTER
UK

Chapter 4A

Catching up with Auntie Varvara

This is an extra chapter to bring everybody up to date with Auntie Varvara's doings. One of the hardest things a Narrator has to do, believe me, is keep everyone informed of what's going on in the lives of people who are, for the moment, out of the main narrative. I thought, when Auntie Varvara set out for two weeks in Transylvania, that in such a short time she would hardly be missed, but ... (and this is the exciting part) SHE DID NOT RETURN! Nor will she before Christmas. Therefore I feel it my duty to put together a kind of patchwork of bits and pieces from her letters, so that you can be part of everything that has happened to her since her departure. It has been no easy task editing the collected letters of Auntie Varvara. She is one of those writers who spill every single thought out on to the page in a rather slipshod fashion. She keeps a diary, and so is well-used to displaying every emotion on paper. She uses too many underlinings and exclamation marks in my opinion, but when once I plucked up courage to tell her so, she pointed out that Queen Victoria was partial to underlinings and exclamation marks, and if something was good enough for Queen

Victoria, then it was good enough for her. I was silenced. Here then are Auntie Varvara's adventures.

'Darlings, This is *the* most amazing place! Up a fantastically steep hill covered in frightfully *brooding* and *sinister-looking* pine trees to our hotel, The Gothic Inn. And you'll never credit this, but guess what the whole place is *absolutely* thick with? That's right! TURRETS! You can hardly turn around without bumping into one ... Went on our first tour today to a couple of local castles. Incredible draughty places, tattered tapestries, mouldy cellars, all exactly as you'd imagine ... There's a most *divine* tour guide called Olaf, with the most beautiful pale cheeks and circles under his eyes, an absolute *mine* of information ... Have made some very good friends on this trip. Best of all are Zenobia Lupino and her brother, Remo. (A *very* unusual name, don't you think?) They have invited me on a teensy jaunt (isn't that a *blissful* way of describing it?) around Europe with them for a few weeks. I *did* feel a little guilty about accepting, knowing how busy you must be in the shop, Eddie, what with Christmas just around the comer, but I'm sure you'll understand ... We have become such *close* companions. I think what drew us together first was the fact that they, too, are vegetarians. Isn't that the *most* thrilling coincidence? We've had such fun exchanging recipes ... So good to speak to you all on the phone last night. Isn't it just MAGIC? The phone, I mean! We are now in Germany, staying with the Lupinos' distant cousins, the Wolff family, in the most Gothic of Gothic houses. Candles beside the bed and everything, all ready for a good exploration of the dark corridors whenever you feel like it ... Poor dear Remo had a bit of a narrow escape the other day. He was just examining a suit of armour in the Grand Hall, and didn't notice that the nails holding up the stag's head on the wall above it had worked themselves loose over the years. I *knew* it was all going to fall on top of him, and sure enough, it nearly did. Luckily I was able to stop it just in time, and think it over to the other side of the room instead, where it did some damage to a rather rickety chair. Remo was most impressed ... and somewhat shaken by the experience ... I'm so gloriously happy. Zenobia and Remo are *so* kind, especially Remo. Tomorrow we are off to Italy. It's where the Lupino family originates, just like ours. Isn't that *an astonishing coincidence?* I enclose a photograph of us taken on one of our outings. Isn't Remo handsome?* I must admit, I'm growing very fond of him! I'm keeping my fingers crossed ... OH, HEAVENLY, BLISSFUL JOY! Remo has declared his love. He loves me. I can hardly believe it.

Will write later when I've taken it in ... Yes, it's true ...
we're *IN LOVE*! I can't describe how marvellous ...'
etc., etc.

From this point, Auntie Varvara's letters become very
boring. It has never ceased to amaze me how those who
are in love can find billions of different ways of saying
the same thing over and over again, but there you are.
Auntie Varvara is in love, just as Filomena foresaw in
the knitting. She will return before Christmas, she tells
us, possibly bringing Remo and his sister for a visit.
Until such time as she reappears, you are to keep an
image of her in your minds, flitting around Europe in
a cloud of Fatal Kiss perfume, from one ancient castle
to another, radiantly happy and joyously *IN LOVE*!
Auntie Varvara's punctuation is catching!

---

* Narrator's note: Remo is a dark and hairy young man with large, rather
pointed teeth. Take my word for it, handsome is not a word that springs to
mind at once, but as someone wisely said: Beauty is in the eye of the beholder.

Chapter 5
The Collins wedding

Have you noticed how often disasters and misfortunes, quarrels and upheavals, bickerings and floods of tears happen at the weekend? It's something I've remarked on many times: how trouble waits quietly until the week's work is done and then hits you with everything it can lay its hands on early on Saturday morning. On this occasion, I'm glad to say, the trouble wasn't happening to the Fantoras, but to the Collinses, our next door neighbours.

We'd known about the wedding for a long time. Dora Collins' little darling, as she called her, whose real name was Lynette, was going to marry a young man called Nick Simpson, a harmless enough fellow, who was believed to have good prospects at the bank where he worked. Almost from the day we'd moved into Azalea Avenue, Dora had been in and out of the house, discussing with Rosie and Filomena such fascinating topics as what everyone was going to have to eat at the reception, where the young couple would be going for their honeymoon, how lucky they were to have found such a nice little flat so cheaply, not to mention the dress, the bridesmaid's outfit, and the composition of the bridal bouquet. I have to admit to not having listened as intently as perhaps I should have done. Many a time, I confess, my eyes had simply closed of their own accord during discussions about the shocking price of satin ribbon and the like. Still, in general we were all kept well-informed. Filomena was called upon to look into her knitting, and pronounced the omens favourable.

'Plenty of very tight cables,' she'd said. 'That's good, winding round one another like that. That shows great devotion. The odd bobble here and there, but that's married life for you, isn't it? Little lovers' tiffs, that's what those are. No, the future looks very bright for the newly-weds, taking it as a whole.' Dora was satisfied.

We should perhaps have expected what happened on Saturday morning, because at supper-time on Friday, Filomena was full of grim warnings.

'Terrible bilious green,' she muttered. 'Violent purple together with flecked orange and black ... No red, thank goodness, but I don't like it, I can tell you. I don't like it at all. And here's a very strange green zigzag flash ... whatever can that be? Something tearing? Someone clawing at something? I hope it isn't you, Ozzy, planning some mischief.'

I ignored that remark as unworthy of an answer, but I did ponder the portents for a while, and tremble slightly when I thought of all those nasty things happening. I knew they would happen, but how and to whom and above all, when? What stopped me from thinking about them any further at that moment was Francesca. She and Rosie had begun to plan Francesca's birthday party. Her birthday was 5th November, Guy Fawkes Night. Planning a party meant Rosie was listening while Francesca told her what kind of party she wanted.

'A tobogganing party,' she said. 'I can make a huge snowstorm in the park, and then we can all slide down the hilly bit, and then when we get home, we can have a barbecue in the garden. I'll make sure it's a sunny afternoon. I don't feel like fireworks this year. I always have fireworks.'

'Don't you think it'll be a little tiring for you, dear, producing a snowstorm in the morning and sunshine in the afternoon?'

'Course not!' Francesca was scornful. 'I can do snowstorms easily now. Shall I show you?'

'No, thank you, dear,' said Rosie quickly. 'I believe you. Well, your birthday's not for another week or so, there's plenty of time.'

'No, there isn't,' Francesca said. I want to take the invitations in on Monday. Can we go and buy some tomorrow?'

'Yes, of course, dear. Now run along and play, and will you please take Leopard down off that shelf, and tell Monkey to come out from under the rug?'

Francesca whistled at Monkey and Leopard, and they followed her out of the room.

That was Friday evening. Saturday morning started pleasantly enough. Everyone was listening to Filomena reading bits of Auntie Varvara's latest letter out loud. I myself was sitting on the window sill in the autumn sunshine. Suddenly we heard a blood-stopping scream from next door. Filomena dropped the letter into her cereal, and although she plucked it out instantly, there were a couple of sentences where the ink had run so badly that we never discovered what they said. Eddie burned his tongue swallowing more hot tea than he'd intended, Bianca dropped her toast, marmalade-side down on the carpet, Francesca leapt to her feet, frightening Monkey and Leopard, who climbed to the top of the dresser and refused to come down for ages. I nearly fell off the window sill.

'Eddie,' said Filomena, 'go at once and see what's happened. It's the wedding today, as you know.'

'I think Rosie ought to go,' said Eddie. 'She's better at dealing with problems than I am.'

Luckily, before the argument had properly got going, we heard a frantic knocking on the front door.

'I'll go,' said Bianca.

'No, me,' said Marco.

'Me too,' said Francesca, and they all three raced out of the room to see who it was. Francesca came back first.

'It's Auntie Dora,' she announced. 'She's crying.'

That was an understatement. Poor Dora almost floated into the kitchen on a wave of tears. They were pouring out of her faster than she could mop them up. She was crying so hard, she couldn't even speak. Rosie knew exactly what to do.

'Now you come and sit down here, Dora,' she said, 'and don't try and speak at all till you've had some of this. You need to calm your nerves.' She had been pouring some pink syrup from a bottle into a small glass as she spoke. Blubbing sounds escaped from Mrs Collins' mouth which I myself couldn't understand, but which must have meant something to Rosie, because she said, 'No, no, it's not brandy, just a little soothing mixture of my own. Just take a little drop, it'll make you feel much better.'

Dora drank. In two seconds, the tears stopped flowing. In four seconds, her nose was clear, in another five, the red blotches round her eyes had disappeared, and in another ten, all the sobs had left her voice and she was speaking quite normally, and – in my opinion – even more cheerfully than she normally spoke.

'That is amazing stuff,' she said. 'Just look at me ... it's like magic. I wasn't fit to be seen, not one minute ago. Why, it's just like magic.'

Rosie smiled mysteriously and said, 'But whatever's the matter? Don't tell me. Lynette's changed her mind. She doesn't want to get married. Is that it?'

Dora laughed. 'Oh no, that's not it at all.'

'Well, what is it, then?' said Eddie.

I could see he was waiting for a chance to leave. For us it was the weekend, but of course the shop still had to open, and it was nine o'clock already.

Dora ticked the morning's disasters off on her fingers.

'First, the baker's van bringing the cake was in a crash this morning. No one was hurt, but the cake was smashed to a pulp.'

'That's the orange and black tweed,' Filomena muttered.

'So,' continued Dora, 'we have no cake and the wedding starts at three o'clock. Then my sister from Rochdale rings up first thing and tells me her kiddies have both got measles, so, no bridesmaid and no page-boy. And just to put the tin lid on it, there's the bouquet all wrapped up in cellophane, lying in the sink in the laundry room, and the cat decides it's claw-sharpening time. Tears the whole lot to shreds. Not one whole petal left in the bunch. I went into the laundry room a few minutes ago and I screamed. I did, honestly. It was like finding a dead body. Well, that was the last straw. After the cake and the kids, I mean, all our hard work gone for nothing. I started crying and until you gave me that drink of yours, Rosie, I didn't think I'd ever be able to stop, I'm that miserable.' She beamed cheerfully at us all.

'Kids with measles,' said Filomena. 'That'll be the bilious green ... and the zigzag is the shredded flowers, of course.'

'You're not to worry about anything,' said Rosie. 'We can solve all of those problems. Eddie, will you be able to provide a bouquet?'

'I should think so,' said Eddie. 'I'll see what I can manage in the shop and I'll bring something back at lunch time. Any special requests?'

'Ooh, you are kind,' said Dora. 'Anything, really. I know Lynette likes spring flowers, but October is October, isn't it? You can't do anything about that.'

Eddie chuckled to himself, and went to put his coat on. I knew what Eddie was happy about. Lynette would get her spring flowers. Eddie had once told me that tulips and daffodils were the quickest and easiest things to grow in the whole world. I watched him leave for the shop, and then turned back to the conversation, which was now all about bridesmaids and page boys.

'Bianca and Marco,' Filomena said, 'we will go now with Dora and try the clothes on. You are lucky to have a grandmother who knows how to do alterations.'

'Oh, I'm sure that won't be necessary,' Dora said. 'Justine and Jason are almost exactly the same ages as you two.'

'But perhaps,' Filomena suggested gently, 'they are shorter or taller. It won't hurt to try.'

'I don't want to be a page boy,' said Marco. 'I'll look silly. I don't like everyone looking at me.'

'Well, I want to be a bridesmaid, so there,' said Bianca, 'so you'll just have to do something you don't want for once.'

'I'm always doing stuff I don't want,' said Marco. 'You always get your way.'

'Stop it, children,' said Rosie. 'We haven't time for all this nonsense. Marco, of course you will be a page-boy – and no disappearing either, or there'll be no party afterwards for you. Understand?'

Marco nodded. When his mother's eyes flashed like that, he knew it was dangerous to defy her. 'All right,' he muttered. 'I suppose it won't be too bad.'

'I want to be a bridesmaid too,' said Francesca.

'But sweetheart,' said Rosie, 'there isn't a dress for you.'

'I'll wear my fairy costume.'

I, for one, was impressed at the way Francesca had worked out all the details.

'It's white and frilly,' she continued. 'And sparkly. I'll look very nice.'

Dora gurgled. 'Oh, do let her. It'll be ever so sweet, really. Lynette'll be pleased too. I know she will.'

Rosie looked doubtful. 'I don't know,' she said. 'She is young and the service might be very long for her. She'll get restless.'

'I won't!' Francesca was indignant. 'I never get restless. If you don't let me, I'll ... I'll ...'

'What'll you do, little poppet?' said Dora.

Francesca smiled winningly. 'I'll set fire to the bridesmaid's dress.'

Dora thought this was the funniest thing she'd ever heard. She rocked backwards and forwards on her chair, and hugged herself as she laughed.

'Just listen to it!' she shrieked. 'The size of it! Going to set fire to a dress, indeed. Well, there's no need for that, Miss Francesca, because you are going to be a bridesmaid, in your fairy dress.'

'Thank you,' said Francesca, happy again now that she had her way. 'I shall go and get it all ready.'

'And you, Bianca and Marco, come with me,' said

Filomena. 'We shall see what needs to be altered. Dora, come, you will lead the way.' Dora rose to her feet, and the small procession filed out of the room.

'Right,' said Rosie to me when they had all gone, 'it's just you and me now, Ozzy. Stand aside a moment and we'll get this cake organized.'

Now, I expect you've seen professional cooks on the television and wondered how it is they manage to achieve such miraculous results without ever spilling a drop of anything at all on their clothes. They have, of course, all the latest technological equipment at their disposal, but Rosie believed in the old ways.

'We won't even use the microwave, Ozzy,' she said. 'This counts as an emergency, I'm afraid.' She clicked her fingers, and a faraway humming noise filled the kitchen. Rosie sat at the head of the table and rather like a conductor telling an orchestra what to play and when and how loudly, she directed operations. I started by trying to follow the action (the eggs and butter beating themselves to fluffiness in the huge bowl, the oven doors opening and shutting by themselves, the spoons dancing out of the drawers when needed), but it hurt my eyes after a while. Everything was going too quickly. I simply couldn't keep up. I closed my eyes for a moment, and when I opened them again, three separate sponge cakes were being enveloped in blankets of white icing and garlands of pink and white sugar roses were being piped round the edges at high speed. Rosie stood up.

'I had a little bride and groom set somewhere,' she said, looking through a drawer. By this time, the iced and flower-spangled layers of wedding cake were climbing on to silver boards and arranging themselves one on top of the other (biggest at the bottom, smallest at the top), with little pillars to keep the layers apart.

'Here we are,' said Rosie, turning to look at the cake on the kitchen table. She put the figures of the bride and groom on to the top layer and stood back.

'Not bad, is it, Ozzy?' she asked me. The humming had stopped, leaving a funny kind of empty space in my head where it used to be. I purred my admiration. We were both so entranced with the cake that neither of us saw Eddie come in.

'Hello, love,' he said to Rosie. 'Where is everyone? Anything tasty for lunch?'

'You'll have to make yourself a sandwich, dear,' said Rosie. 'I haven't had a minute all morning to think about lunch.' That was certainly true, but it didn't account for Eddie's reaction. He turned quite white and then bright scarlet and sat down hurriedly in the nearest chair.

'Whatever's the matter?' said Rosie, quite anxiously. 'I'll do you a sandwich if you don't think you can manage it.'

'No, it's not that,' said Eddie. 'It's the flowers for the bouquet. I forgot entirely about them. We've been run off our feet in the shop. I literally haven't had a second. Oh heavens, whatever shall I do?'

'It's one o'clock now. You've got about an hour and a half. I'll make you a sandwich and you get cracking. Are there any empty pots in the greenhouse?'

Eddie shook his head miserably. 'Everything's chock-a-block,' he said. 'I've got all sorts growing down there, but no flowers.'

Rosie sighed. 'Oh well, just this once as it's an emergency. Use the bath and this sink and the one in the utility room, and if you need another, you'll have to go up and use Filomena's, though I don't think she'll take too kindly to that.'

'No, no, three'll do. One for tulips, one for daffs, and one for narcissi. Will that be enough, do you think?'

'She's lucky to get that. Go on, get started. I'll bring your sandwich in a minute.'

'Come on then, Ozzy,' said Eddie. 'You come with me. Do you know, there are people in the world who have a complete rest on Saturdays? Isn't that an astonishing fact? Not me. Overtime for me.'

One hour later, it was time to pick the flowers. Eddie

had put two inches of his Miracle Compost in the bottom of the bath, and now there were more daffodils in it than most parks can manage in a year. In the sink in the kitchen, red and yellow and pink tulips stood shoulder to shoulder, like a regiment of guards. The utility room was fragrant with narcissi.

'Oh, Eddie,' Rosie sighed, 'did you need quite so many? We only want one bouquet for one bride.'

'I'll take the rest to the shop, dear, don't worry. They'll keep till Monday, never fear.'

'Well, just quickly pick a bunch for Lynette and we'll leave the clearing-up till afterwards. We ought to be getting dressed now, or we'll be late.' She ran upstairs.

'It's a hard life, Ozzy,' Eddie said, as he bent to pick the best tulips. 'And no mistake.'

'You've eaten,' said Marco to Bianca at the reception, 'fourteen of those biscuit thingies with prawns on top.'

'Have not,' said Bianca, popping another into her mouth.

'You have,' said Marco. 'I've been counting.'

'I'm telling Ozzy,' said Bianca loftily, changing the subject, 'all about the wedding. About how pretty the bride looked.'

'She didn't look all that pretty,' said Marco. 'She

looked just like she always looks, only in a white dress with a sticky-out skirt and a veil.'

'Shut up,' said Bianca. 'You know nothing about it. She looked lovely and so did I. I could hear people saying "Ooh" and "Aah" as we walked up the aisle.'

'That was probably for Francesca,' said Marco, 'or even me. I heard people saying how handsome I was.'

'Anyway,' said Bianca, not wishing to dwell on Marco's handsomeness, 'it all went very well. The flowers, everyone was talking about the flowers. They couldn't get over daffs in October. I heard someone say that they'd been flown in from Florida by Concorde. Eddie's ever so pleased.'

The cake, too, had been very well received. Not much of it was left, only some pale yellow crumbs and fragments of pink and white sugar roses. The Collins' house was full of guests, all talking at once. Bianca and Marco had been given identical digital watches as their present from the groom, and they were happily occupied pushing one button after another and seeing what happened. Francesca's present (and not a word to her, but I suspect it once belonged to Lynette – Francesca was, after all, a last-minute addition to the ceremony) was a pretty, heart-shaped locket made of silver. Strangely, though, this present did not seem to have made her very happy. The corners of her mouth were turned firmly downwards, and I could see a frown gathering between her eyebrows which did not bode well for the Collins' rather inflammable-looking curtains. I saw Rosie making her way through the crowds to see what was the matter, and my curiosity got the better of me, I confess. I followed her.

'Francesca, darling, there you are,' said Rosie. 'Why, what's the matter, lovey? Aren't you feeling well?'

Francesca burst into tears. 'You forgot,' she cried. 'You forgot to get my party invitations and now I won't be able to take them in on Monday. It's dark now, and I know all the shops are closed on Sunday.' Her shoulders shook with sobs. Rosie took out a handkerchief.

'Francesca, blow your nose at once! I'm ashamed of you. One wouldn't think that you were nearly six. Now, where do we buy party invitations?'

'At Mr Ashworth's shop.'

'And what kind of shop is that?'

'It's a newsagent's.'

'Quite right. And what kind of shop is always open on a Sunday morning to sell Sunday newspapers?'

'A newsagent's.'

'Well, now,' said Rosie, 'can we go to Mr Ashworth's shop tomorrow and get the invitations?'

'Yes.' Francesca hung her head and sniffed quietly.

'And can you take them in to school on Monday?'

'Yes.'

'Then come and see Lynette and Nick going off on their honeymoon. Everyone's going out to wave at the car. Come on ... you might catch the bride's bouquet.'

'What does it mean if I do?' asked Francesca.

'It means you'll be the next bride.'

This idea clearly appealed to Francesca, because she rushed off after the other guests and took up her position near the gate. Then a most unusual thing happened. Just as Lynette tossed her bouquet into the air, a gust of wind caught it and lifted it higher and higher. It flew in through the half-open skylight of our house. Everyone laughed and made jokes about there being no weddings for a while, and then forgot about it altogether. I found it very much later that same evening, when I went in to have a small snooze on Auntie Varvara's bed. There they were: daffodils, narcissi, and tulips lying in the most orderly way imaginable right in the very centre of the lace-trimmed pillow. I began to ponder the significance of this, but working out its deeper meaning became too much for me and I fell asleep.

EXTRACT FROM MY FILES NO. 6:

Francesca's Party Invitation

COME TO MY PARTY!

On: Saturday 5th November

at: 2 p.m.

meet at: Hillbrow Park, near the duckpond

collect from: 58, Azalea Avenue

Barton Bridge Estate

Please bring any sleds, toboggans or skis if you have them. Also gloves and woolly hats. The weather will be cold and full of surprises.

RSV.P Tel: 454-3714

Chapter 6
Francesca's party

'When can we go, Mum?' asked Francesca. 'Can we go straight after breakfast?'

'Well, how long will it take you?'

'Quite long,' said Francesca. 'It's going to take lots and lots of snow to cover up all those hilly bits.'

'An hour?'

'I expect so.'

Rosie smiled. 'Then we certainly don't have to leave the house straight after breakfast. We'll go down to the park at twelve o'clock. That'll give us a bit of extra time if we need it.'

They were discussing the snowstorm. It seemed to me (though I am not well up in meteorological matters) that it was going to be quite an undertaking for a slip of a child like Francesca. How wrong I was! I jumped into the van when, at twelve o'clock precisely, Rosie and Francesca set off for the park to prepare the ground. Because I am naturally curious, I wanted to see how it was done. I don't know quite what I'd imagined, but certainly something more spectacular than what actually happened. I stayed in the van, watching out of the back window. I did not wish to be snowed upon, and I had an excellent view of everything. Francesca simply strode over the ground with her arms above her head and a deep frown on her face. For a while, nothing happened at all. Several people looked sideways at what they considered to be a strange sight: a little girl in a bright red anorak stomping around with her arms above her head, muttering under her breath.

It was a grey, cool sort of a day. Not quite wet, but with a thin, misty moisture hanging in the air. Then, after I had practically given up hope, storm clouds began to mass overhead. Mauve and deep blue-grey they were, hanging low in the sky, and pressing themselves down over the grassy slopes of this part of the park. Quite suddenly, the snow started falling. Before long, the air around us was thick with snow. I could hardly see Rosie and Francesca through the scattering white. There was a clock set in the dashboard of the van. I timed the snowstorm. For exactly forty-three minutes a blizzard blew. The snow settled on the ground like sugar being sifted on to strawberries, then it grew thicker and thicker until all that I could see was a desert of white dips and dunes and hollows. When Rosie and Francesca got back into the van, it was ten past one.

'Exactly an hour, Francesca,' said Rosie. 'Well done! Now let's go home and change into our skiing clothes.'

I was a little worried about leaving the snow to its

own devices. What if it melted? What if everyone else in the park trampled it to slush? I told my worries to Francesca.

'Don't worry, Ozzy,' she whispered as she stroked my ears, 'there's a special kind of force, like a sort of magnet in reverse. People will come and look all round the edges, but they can't come in unless I let them. It's my own personal weather, you see, and as for melting, well, it doesn't change until I tell it to, do you understand?'

I purred softly at her and closed my eyes, but not before I'd seen, just on the very edges of the snowy area, a long line of curious people staring at this sudden miracle, wondering why it was they couldn't get near enough to touch it. They would all go home and write letters to the local paper. Perhaps there would even be a headline: 'Freak Snowstorm in Local Park'.

I have to confess that I did not go to the winter sports section of the party. Devoted though I am to Francesca, my idea of fun is certainly *not* trudging up snowy slopes and sliding down them at top speed on a polished piece of wood. Therefore I shall leave you to imagine all by yourselves the squeals of joy, the bobble-hats and stripey scarves and, above all, the general amazement at the sight of so much of the park suddenly inches deep in thick, soft, and extremely cold snow.

No, I chose the easier option, I must admit, and sat in the dining-room listening to Bianca and Marco planning the entertainment. This was to be a play, and it was going to be performed by Candy, Sandy, Mandy and Shandy, with a couple of Marco's soldiers acting the hero and the villain, and a toy dinosaur playing the dragon. The children had turned the serving-hatch between the kitchen and the dining-room into a stage. The kitchen part was backstage, and a blue cloth separated it from the front of the stage. There, on the ledge that normally held dishes ready to be brought to the table, all the dolls, brought to life by Bianca, were getting ready for the performance.

'They'll be back from the park soon,' said Bianca, 'and then there's the barbecue. You're all on after that. Sandy, do you remember your words?'

'Of course I do,' said Sandy, 'only I don't see why I have to be the Horrible Queen. Why can't I be the Beautiful Princess instead of Candy?'

'Because you're the oldest. And that's the story, anyway. Marco wrote the story. Besides, the Queen becomes nicer in the end.'

'But she's horrid at first.' Sandy stuck her pink nose in the air. 'And I don't see why we have to have a dragon in the story. Or a fight. Boys always put in fights.'

'It makes it more exciting,' said Marco. 'That's why. And dragons are in lots of fairy stories, and anyhow my dinosaur likes acting, exactly as you do, so there. Now just try it once more before they all come back and we have to stop.'

'Well, I don't care,' said Sandy, who liked to have the last word. 'I've got the shiniest dress. Even Candy's dress doesn't glitter like mine does!'

The barbecue was taking place in the back garden. It was four o'clock, and Francesca had managed to put a little extra sparkle into the last of the November sunlight, so that all the guests could eat their chicken and beefburgers without feeling the cold. Filomena was walking round among the children pouring out lemonade, and Rosie was getting the cake (a chocolate one in the shape of a six) ready for the candle-blowing ceremony. Eddie was standing beside the barbecue, flipping burgers from one side to the other and making sure all the chicken was evenly brown.

'Nothing worse,' he said to me, 'than food charred on one side and raw on the other. Can you think of anything worse? Now me,' he gave a couple of burgers a deft push with a long fork, 'I'm a perfectionist.

Everything coming off this grill will be done to a turn!'

And it was. I can vouch for it, because I spent a very happy time eating up the bits of this and that which people kept dropping on to the grass. After a while, the sun sank below the horizon, dusk fell, and there was nothing left to eat anywhere. Bianca's voice rang out. She had opened the french window leading from the dining-room into the garden, and come out on to the patio.

'Ladies and gentlemen, boys and girls,' she said. 'It is time to come inside and watch the entertainment.'

All the children rushed for the door. 'One at a time and sit down quietly on the floor,' Bianca continued. 'You are going to see a short play.'

When all the children had settled down, Marco closed the door and drew the curtains.

'This play is called *The Princess and the Dragon*,' said Bianca, 'and Marco wrote it. It's acted by my dolls, Sandy, Candy, and Mandy and Shandy the dog is also in it. So are two of Marco's soldiers and his dinosaur. Are you ready?'

'Yes!' shouted all Francesca's friends, so Marco touched a switch, the dining room grew dark and everyone fell silent. The only light shone through the serving hatch from the kitchen, illuminating what was supposed to be the bedroom of Princess Griselda, played by Candy.

It was a touching story. Princess Griselda was being forced by her greedy mother, Queen Esmeralda (who wanted to be the richest person in the world), to marry Captain Jim, who was wealthy and wicked. Only her pet dragon, Dermott, could help her escape. Dermott blew fire all over Captain Jim, who ran away in terror, and Griselda escaped to a cottage in the forest. There she met a woodcutter called Igor, who had a dog (that was Shandy!) and they married and had a baby (that was Mandy!). Captain Jim fought Igor when he found his cottage in the forest, saying that the winner would take Griselda as his wife. Captain Jim was beaten by Igor in the fight and ran back to tell Esmeralda what had happened to her daughter. Esmeralda said, 'Oh well, never mind about being rich, let's go and visit them.' So she and Captain Jim became nice in the end and everyone lived happily ever after.

I, of course, had seen the play in rehearsal, so I stepped out into the garden again to help with the clearing up ... that is, the finding of further morsels in the grass. I was padding along with my nose near the ground when I found a collection of labels torn from tins of fruit and held together by a paper clip. It seemed to me a very peculiar thing to find, and so I decided to take them to Eddie. He would know what they were. I picked them up and went to find him. He was putting the barbecue away.

'What's this, then, Ozzy?' he said. 'Peaches, pears, apricots, mandarins, guavas, lychees ... Oh, I see, someone's been collecting these. Probably get a free pepper-mill or something when you've got enough. I should get rid of it, if I were you. Half of the labels are torn, and the other half are filthy dirty. No one could possibly want them now.' Eddie turned back to his barbecue. I took the labels, intending to throw them into the dustbin, when Eddie came racing after me.

'Ozzy, Ozzy, let's have those labels a minute!' He took them from me and looked at them again. 'Ozzy,' he breathed, 'this may be it ... the breakthrough I've been waiting for! Don't you see? These labels make up a Fruit Salad! Oh, Ozzy, wouldn't a Fruit Salad Tree be fantastic? Can't you picture it? I'd be famous. Everyone would come from far and wide to ask me how I did it. I might even be on *Gardeners' Question Time* on the radio! All my customers would ask for my autograph, to say nothing of buying more in the shop. Yes, yes, I know it's mad. I know they're only paper labels with pictures on them, but I'm going to try it. Yes, I am. I've tried nearly everything else.' He turned, and hurried down to the greenhouse in the dark, and I followed him.

'Look here, Ozzy,' he said, 'we'll just put these papers

at the bottom of a flowerpot, cover them with Miracle Compost and keep our fingers crossed.' All around him on the tables and shelves of the greenhouse were various pots bearing Fruit Salad Tree experiments that had come to nothing. Eddie had tried to grow his tree from seeds, from cuttings, from the fruits themselves ... in truth, the only thing he hadn't tried were tins and paper labels. Some of his experiments had half-worked. He had managed to grow a lemons-and-oranges tree, but that, as he pointed out sadly, was a long way from a fruit salad. There was also the grapevine with no grapes, the banana tree with nothing but bananas on it ... in short, nothing that one could accurately call a salad of any kind.

'Now don't tell a soul about this, Ozzy old chap. They'll think we've taken leave of our senses.'

I nodded, of course, but I have to say that I, too, thought he'd taken leave of his senses, and as for including me in this lunacy, well, I had no words to express my indignation. I curled up on a distant shelf and closed my eyes, pretending to ignore completely everything that Eddie was doing.

* * *

The guests were all leaving when Eddie and I returned to the house. I heard one little girl say, 'I don't think it's magic. I just think they've got a special kind of puppet, that's all. I think it all works by electricity.'

'But how could puppets know the words Marco wrote, all off by heart like that?' said a second girl.

'Some of them didn't know the words very well, though, did they? The dragon or dinosaur or whatever he was forgot his altogether and asked Bianca what happened next.'

'There you are then,' said the second girl. 'It proves it's magic. Electrical things don't ask you for help when they break down.'

'I don't believe in magic,' said the first girl firmly. 'I expect it's done by remote control.'

They followed their mothers out of the gate and were swallowed up by the darkness.

Are you the kind of person who likes to know what people had for their birthday? I know I am, so I will give you a list of what Francesca received:

Any number of felt-tip pen sets

A couple of scrapbooks

1 jigsaw puzzle

4 books

1 Sindy doll in a bride's dress (Francesca had wanted one of these since the Collins announced their wedding!)

1 pencil-case.

Francesca had all these things around her on the kitchen floor and while everybody else cleared up after the party, she was looking at them, one after another.

'Must you do that here?' said Rosie. 'It's very hard for us, walking around you all the time. Put all that stuff on the table. Help her, Bianca and Marco.'

Bianca and Marco and Francesca moved all the presents. Filomena came in just at that moment with both hands hidden behind her back.

'What do you think I've got here, Francesca?' she asked.

Francesca considered. 'It can't be my present from you because I'm wearing that. I love it, Filomena.'

'I'm glad you do. I specially made it in stripes of ice cream colours because I know you like ice cream. It is a magic cardigan, naturally. Whenever you wear it, there'll be ice cream around for supper. What's the pudding for supper tomorrow, Rosie?'

'Ice cream and chocolate sauce,' said Rosie.

'There you are! What did I tell you?' Filomena chuckled. 'But you still haven't guessed what I've got behind me here.'

'I know!' Francesca jumped up from her chair. 'It's a present from Auntie Varvara! Is it? I thought she'd forgotten.'

'No, she hasn't and you're quite right, it *is* a present

from Auntie Varvara. But there's something else as well. Something you've forgotten.'

'Oh, do let me see Auntie Varvara's present,' Francesca jumped up and down, 'and then I'll guess what the other thing is … two things! Oh, I can't wait!'

Auntie Varvara had sent a lovely little pale-grey velvet bat. It wasn't exactly a stuffed animal, more a lightly quilted one, with beautiful wings and a sweet expression on its face. Auntie Varvara's card said, 'This is a bat from Transylvania, just like the ones that flutter about in Dracula's castle at twilight. Isn't he sweet? His name is Boris. Happy birthday, Francesca dear. See you soon. Love from Auntie Varvara.'

'He's beautiful!' Francesca squeaked. 'Bring him to life, Bianca. Let him fly around a bit!'

'Not here, please, girls,' said Rosie, 'and not now. Bats are the last thing I need while I'm trying to clean up the kitchen.'

'But he's not just bats,' Francesca wailed. 'He's Beautiful Boris.'

'I don't care if he's Magnificent Montmorency,' said Rosie. 'Just keep him out of my kitchen, that's all I ask. He's very cute and cuddly, I grant you that, but bats are Gothic and I'm not having Gothic in my kitchen and that's final.'

Francesca sighed and picked Beautiful Boris up and stroked him. 'Never mind, Boris,' she said softly, 'you can have a good fly around in our room before bedtime.'

'Talking of bedtime,' said Filomena, 'you still haven't guessed what this is, have you?' She brought out a square-ish parcel from behind her back. Francesca shook her head. 'Open it, then,' said Filomena. 'I must say, I *am* surprised at you, not remembering.'

'It's a cushion,' said Francesca. 'It's lovely, Filomena. Thank you. Look at all the different colours, browns and greens and greys, and lots of little bows ... oh, they're like butterflies. It's really beautiful. I shall put it on my bed.'

'You *still* don't know what it is, do you?' Filomena tutted in amazement.

'It's a cushion,' said Francesca.

'It's more than that,' said Filomena. 'It's a Dream Cushion.'

'A Dream Cushion? What's that?'

'It's what I'm making with my class at school. Starting on Wednesday. You choose a place to dream about. In your case, Francesca, it's a splendid forest, full of butterflies and rays of sunlight through the trees, and thick moss and mauve flowers. You collect wools in all the right colours and you make a cushion. If you put it on your bed at night, then you dream about the place. You can make lots of different ones. It's probably boring, dreaming about the same place all the time, night after night.'

'Does it really, truly work?' Francesca wanted to know.

'Of course it works. It's powerful magic,' said Filomena.

'Thank you,' said Francesca, hugging Filomena. 'It's been a wonderful birthday.'

The next morning, Francesca looked sulky.

'I didn't dream about forests,' she complained.

'Oh yes, you did, dear,' said Filomena. 'Pass the cereal, please.'

'I didn't. At least, I can't remember dreaming at all.'

'There you are then,' said Filomena calmly. 'You dreamed about a forest, even though you can't remember your dream now. One quite often can't recall one's dreams, but I promise you, you dreamed about a forest. It's guaranteed when you put your Dream Cushion on your bed.'

Francesca grinned. 'It's a cheat, Filomena, isn't it? If no one can remember what they dreamed ...'

'It doesn't mean to say they didn't dream of what they were supposed to,' said Filomena firmly. '*They* may not know, but *I* do, because of my age and experience. Take it from me, you dreamed about forests last night.

It was a wonderful dream.'

Francesca sighed. 'If you say so,' she said, and thought about it silently right to the end of breakfast.

EXTRACT FROM MY FILES NO. 7:

My Cat by Francesca

<u>My Cat</u> by Francesca Fantora.

My cat is called Ozzy. He is fat and black. He can talk. He sleeps a lot. He eats a lot. He knows everything.
I love Ozzy.

Chapter 7

A visit to the art gallery

Wednesday was Filomena's day for being a teacher. Every Wednesday she would appear at breakfast with her hair in a teacher-like bun instead of a plait and wearing what she considered to be teacher clothes – a sensible tweedy skirt, a plain beige blouse, and a lacy cardigan the colour of pease pudding.

'You look horrible,' said Rosie.

'I look suitable,' said Filomena. 'The children take me seriously when I look like this.'

'You're enjoying yourself enormously, aren't you?' said Eddie. 'At the school, I mean.'

'It makes a change,' said Filomena, 'and a change, as you know, is as good as a rest. Come on, Bianca and Marco, it's time to go.'

They walked down the road together towards Otter Street, carrying their lunch boxes. Filomena was not very pleased to be using an old box of Francesca's with pictures of a dark-grey rat called Roland all over it, but agreed that it was hardly worth buying a new lunch box, just for one day a week.

'We're starting properly today,' she said to Bianca and Marco. 'Starting our cushions.'

'Whatever have you been doing for the last few weeks then?' Bianca wanted to know.

'Teaching half the children to knit, for the most part. That took a lot of doing, but they're getting on very well now.'

'Boys as well?' Marco sounded surprised.

Filomena flashed him a warning glance. 'And why not, I should like to know?'

'No reason,' said Marco quickly. I just wondered.'

Filomena snorted. 'Then, naturally, we had to do all the collection and sorting of the wools. Then every child had to plan a cushion, and today we're ready to begin. I think we should all be finished by Christmas if we're lucky. What are you doing today? Wasn't there something arranged?'

'Not for me,' said Marco sadly. 'Bianca's class is going to the art gallery, lucky things.'

'I expect it'll be boring,' said Bianca.

'No, it won't,' said Marco. 'It'll be good. I wish I could come.'

'I'll try and bring you something back. A postcard, or something,'

They turned into the school gates. Bianca and Marco watched as Filomena strode off towards the staffroom, swinging her lunch box. As she walked, a crowd of children gathered around her, running from every corner of the playground to follow her. Marco sighed.

'Have a good time at the art gallery,' he said and turned towards his classroom.

'Come with us,' Bianca said. 'Come on, quick! Go into the cloakroom and make yourself invisible. Hang your bag on a hook. I'll go and tell Mr Weedon you're coming in at dinner-time. It's those bad teeth of yours again,' she grinned. 'Go on. Hurry. Wait at the gate till you see me getting on to the coach.' She ran off and Marco disappeared into the cloakroom.

Wednesday was Eddie's favourite day.

'Closing day for the shop, Ozzy, children at school, my mother at school, my wife at a coffee morning, even my sister gallivanting round Europe ... it's just us, Ozzy. You and me and the greenery. Isn't that splendid?'

I muttered agreement and settled myself down for a sleep while Eddie pottered around the greenhouse. He passed the odd remark to the plants as he went about his work, and sometimes I thought I caught the small answering rustles of new leaves, and the quiet whispering of petals. I was very nearly asleep when I heard a distant rumbling and felt a slight vibration in the shelf. At first I thought it was trains, shaking the greenhouse about, but when I opened my eyes I saw that the flowerpot in which Eddie had planted the wrappers from all those tins of fruit was wobbling about as though something were trapped inside it, trying to escape.

'Look, Ozzy,' shouted Eddie, 'something's going on in that pot!' We both watched in silence as a small silvery tendril poked out of the earth.

'I can't believe this, Ozzy,' said Eddie. 'It's growing so fast ... and look, it's not like a plant at all ... more like an arrangement of silver wires. What *is* going on?'

'It's got lumps all over it,' I said. 'It's like a silver tree with these little lumps growing on all the silver branches.' The trembling and vibrating of the pot had stopped.

'I don't think it's going to do anything else today, do you?' asked Eddie.

I shook my head. What it had already done had disturbed my morning snooze quite a bit. I was heartily glad that the pot and the surrounding shelf had ceased to move. Now I could go back to sleep. Eddie was rubbing his chin thoughtfully as I closed my eyes.

'Those lumps,' he said, 'are somewhat of a mystery. Are they, do you think, going to blossom? And if they are, then into what, I wonder?'

* * *

'This,' said Filomena, 'is going to be fun. Has everyone cast on? Have you got your wool ready? Simon? Nicola? Why not, Zoe? What do you mean, you can't – after all my hard work.' Filomena sighed. 'Well, wait till the others have started and then I'll come and help you, dear. Everyone ready? Then you may begin to knit.'

Twenty-eight pairs of needles began to click in unison. Twenty-eight different combinations of coloured wool began to arrange themselves in knobbly ridges, as twenty-eight separate dreams started to grow.

'Now, Zoe,' said Filomena, 'let's start you off. I'll do the casting-on and the first couple of rows, and then do you think you can manage on your own?'

Zoe nodded and watched in wonder as the old lady's needles moved in and out of the wool so quickly that she could hardly see them.

'There you are, child,' Filomena said after a few moments. 'Now you can get on, can't you?'

Zoe turned her attention to the fairground colours she had chosen for her cushion: red and gold and white. Filomena walked around the classroom, stopping here and there to pick up dropped stitches and sort out tangles and knots, but her mind was far away. She was thinking about her own work, now lying folded up in a basket at 58, Azalea Avenue. Lately she had been knitting flashes of that very particular blue-green that means weddings, and last night the blue-green of weddings had shaped itself into the closely-twisted cables of devotion ... it had to be Varvara and that wolfish young man, Remo. Filomena had said nothing to anybody, but she had recognized some of the names. The Lupinos were a very famous family of Italian werewolves. *It's not*, thought Filomena, *that I've anything against werewolves as such, but whether they make the best husbands in the world ... Still, he is a vegetarian, so there is no real danger to anyone, I suppose. In all probability, hairiness is his worst problem ...*

'Please, Miss, all my stitches have fallen off the needle,' said Zoe, and Filomena ran to help, all thoughts of Varvara forgotten for the moment.

Bianca and her friends, Jenny, Joanne, Tania, Sarah and Anahita were having a giggly time on the coach on the way to the art gallery. Marco (invisible) was standing right behind the driver pretending to drive the coach with him. The girls were sucking sweets and Marco wished that he could be visible and have one too. He sighed. Perhaps he could get Bianca to keep him one for later.

'Now, children,' said Bianca's teacher, Mrs Dawes, as they stood in the entrance to the City Art Gallery, 'you must be very quiet and orderly at all times. We are going to be looking today at the Pre-Raphaelite paintings, to help us with our class project on Victorian life. Up the stairs now, and turn left.'

The children trooped obediently after Mrs Dawes. Marco liked the marble floors, and the thick pillars decorated with garlands of carved and gilded fruit and flowers.

Bianca made straight for the Pre-Raphaelite room, and her friends followed her.

'I don't know where all the others are,' said Bianca.

'They're being slow,' said Tania, 'and looking at everything for ages.'

'But this is easily the best room,' said Jenny.

'I like that stormy picture next door,' said Anahita.

'Some of the pictures in here are really ace,' said Sarah. 'There's people playing music, and chatting and there's all kinds of animals: dogs and sheep and a cat and a peacock and even a snake. Look, in the Adam and Eve picture.'

'I like that one,' said Bianca, pointing to a picture showing four girls standing round a high pile of autumn leaves.

'What are you waiting for?' said a voice near Bianca's ear.

'Marco! I'd forgotten all about you. What do you

mean?'

'I mean, all the others are busy. Go on ... have a bit of fun.'

'Should I?'

'Yes, go on. I dare you.'

Bianca walked quickly round the room. 'There,' she said, 'there's not time to fix everything, but I've done a few odds and ends.'

The first thing that happened was that the whole room was filled with music; lutes and dulcimers in at least three paintings were being sweetly played. Unfortunately, the bleating of a flock of sheep from one picture, the barking of two separate dogs, and the cry of a peacock nearly drowned the songs. A small black cat (which had been perched on top of a baby's cradle floating on a rush of water) jumped down out of the picture it belonged in, and began to chase the leaves that were now blowing about all over the place.

'Look!' shouted Joanne. 'All the leaves have come out of the picture!'

'And so has the cat!' said Jenny. 'How did that happen? It's real magic. Look!'

A small boy with a whip and top was running up and down on the shiny wooden floor towards the corner where a painting of the queen in her parlour, eating bread and honey, came to life for just long enough to allow the hungry-looking monarch time to snatch one more bite. The girls from the autumn leaves picture had come out of their frame, and were dancing to the music of a song sung by two beautiful ladies, with twists of red-gold hair curling round their necks. The turquoise serpent from the Adam and Eve picture had slid down from the apple tree and was making its way towards a carriage containing a little girl called Madeline Scott.

Suddenly a voice like thunder said, 'What is the meaning of this pandemonium?' It was Mrs Dawes. Bianca squeezed her eyes tight shut for an instant and then opened them again.

'The meaning of what, please, Miss?' she asked innocently.

Mrs Dawes blinked and surveyed the silence and order of the Pre-Raphaelite Room in front of her. She took a deep breath. I've been overdoing it, she said to herself. I could have sworn I heard barking and bleating and the sound of singing voices and lutes. And I could also have sworn ... no, that's impossible, but I thought, I really *did* think I saw girls dancing in long dark skirts, and a small black kitten, and a blue snake and all those leaves ... the whole room had been full of red and gold leaves.

'Pick up those two leaves over there, Anahita dear,' said Mrs Dawes shakily. 'You must have brought them in on your shoes. Why are you all giggling? Hurry up now, children.' She turned and strode into the next room.

'I'd like you to have a look at this very beautiful painting by Turner. It's called *Pas de Calais.* And this is a wonderful storm over here ... can't you just feel it?'

The class filed past Mrs Dawes as she stood gazing at the dark water in the gold frame. Bianca couldn't resist it.

'Don't you think you've done enough?' Marco whispered.

'Just the weeniest bit,' Bianca whispered back over her shoulder. She watched as Mrs Dawes stepped hurriedly back from the painting.

'Please, Miss, is anything wrong?'

'No, no, nothing,' said Mrs Dawes. She was thinking, I'll be glad when the Christmas holidays arrive. I felt the spray of the sea water on my face, I know I did. She closed her eyes and thought of cups of tea. She would not, she felt, be taking another party of children out for quite some time.

In the entrance hall once more, and feeling light-hearted with relief because this particular school outing was nearly over, Mrs Dawes said, 'If anyone would like to buy a postcard in the gallery shop, we still have a little time left.'

A wave of children gathered, ready to break over the racks of postcards. Bianca started to go with the others, wanting to look for the 'Autumn leaves' picture, when she felt something pulling at her skirt. She knew who it was at once.

'Stop it, Marco,' she hissed. 'I want to buy a postcard.'

'Later,' he whispered. 'You've got to go back to that room. Something awful's happened.'

'What?'

'You didn't put everything back right.'

'What are you rabbiting on about?'

Marco sighed. 'It's the black kitten.'

'On the baby's cradle. I remember. It was sweet. It looked like Ozzy, a bit. Not so fat, and younger, of course.'

'It's not on the baby's cradle. It's in with those girls piling up the leaves.'

'Well, no one will notice, will they?' Bianca said.

'Bianca, don't be silly, of course people will notice. You've got to come and put that kitten back. Now.'

'Well, how? Any brilliant ideas?'

'Say you left your purse there, or something.'

Bianca went over to Mrs Dawes. 'Please, Miss, can I go back to that room? I dropped my purse there, and now I can't buy a postcard.'

'Oh dear,' said Mrs Dawes. 'I suppose so, but really, Bianca, what a silly thing to do. Not a bit like you. Hurry up now. We have to be on the coach very soon.'

Bianca clattered up the stone steps and through the rooms that led to the Pre-Raphaelite Room, slowing down a little as she went past the attendant.

'I've come to get my purse,' she explained to him. 'I dropped it in there.'

The attendant was unsurprised. 'School parties,' he muttered. 'They're all the same.'

Bianca looked carefully at the 'Autumn leaves' picture. The black kitten was curled up beside the pile of leaves. It looked very happy.

'I'm sorry, Cat,' she said. 'I've got to put you back up there, even though you like it better down here.' The kitten jumped down out of the frame and into Bianca's arms. 'There you go ...' Bianca waited until he had perched himself back on to the baby's cradle, and then hurried out of the room.

'Thank you very much,' she said to the attendant on the way out. 'I've found my purse.'

'There wasn't a cat in there, was there?' he said. 'I thought I heard miaowing.'

'A cat?' said Bianca. 'Oh, no. Only in the picture.'

The attendant shook his head. The miaowing wasn't the only noise he'd heard this morning. Perhaps, he thought to himself, I ought to take early retirement.

Down in the entrance hall, Marco was waiting.

'Did you fix it?' he whispered.

'Yes,' said Bianca. 'Now I'm going to get my postcard.'

'And what kind of day have you had, children?' said Rosie at supper. 'Didn't you go to the art gallery, Bianca?'

'Mmmm,' said Bianca, whose mouth was full.

'Wasn't it interesting?'

'It was OK,' said Bianca. 'I'd rather have gone to see that man they've found who's been buried in a marsh for years and years.'

Filomena frowned. 'You do have bloodthirsty tendencies, Bianca. Remember, please, my remarks about flaunting your gifts. It's very vulgar. Why are you giggling, Marco?'

'I don't know,' said Marco, still giggling.

'Then kindly cease. You will all be pleased,' she continued, 'to know that 4 B's Dream Cushions are progressing satisfactorily. You will also, I think, be interested to learn that the knitting is showing distinct signs of a wedding.'

'Varvara and that Remo!' squealed Rosie. Filomena nodded.

'I can be a bridesmaid again. Goody!' said Francesca.

'Well,' said Eddie, 'that'd be a turn-up for the books. Varvara getting married. Doesn't anyone want to know what I've grown today?'

'Go on,' said Marco. 'Tell us.'

'It's a silver tree.'

'Really?' said Francesca. 'Proper, real silver?'

'No, no,' said Eddie, 'just some shiny, silvery metal. More like aluminium.'

'Oh.' Francesca was disappointed.

'But it's got lumps,' said Eddie, 'and I think, I really do think, that the lumps may blossom into something.'

'What'll they blossom into?' Francesca wanted to know.

'Ah,' said Eddie, 'that is still a secret. We will have to wait and see.'

'I *hate* waiting and seeing,' said Francesca. 'Is it ice cream tonight?'

Rosie groaned. 'It doesn't matter what I make, you always want ice cream and you generally get it. Go on.'

Francesca smiled and went to open the freezer.

EXTRACT FROM MY FILES NO. 8:

Filomena's Dream Cushion Pattern.

A Dream Cushion can be any size you like. If you grow tired or bored while knitting it, it can become a Dream Cushion for one of your dolls or teddy bears. If it gets really large, it may even become a Dream Pillow.

You will need:

> Knitting needles.
>
> Lots of bits of wool.
>
> Leftovers from other people's knitting.
>
> Scraps of this and that.
>
> Anything you can collect.

REMEMBER

Thin needles + thin wool = small Dream Cushions.

Thick needles + thick wool = bigger Dream Cushions.

You will also need bits of cut-up laddered tights or clean rags to fill your cushion and make it nice and plump, but you can leave that till the end. The tights must be washed and dried before you cut them up, otherwise you will have a smelly cushion and dream of dirty feet all night long!

Every row is done in Knit stitch. This is called Garter Stitch.

The most important part: what you want to dream about.

Choose the kind of place you'd like your dream to take

place in. For example, the seaside, a forest or jungle, under the sea, outer space, a fairground – wherever you like.

METHOD

1) Collect bits of wool in colours that suit your 'place'. Forests will be greens and browns and greys, with bits of mauve for mushrooms. Under the sea will be every shade of blue and green with pinks for corals and shells. The seaside will be yellows and oranges and browns and clear blue. When you've got enough bits in the right colours, join them all together to make a big ball, winding them up as you go. The more wool you have, the bigger your cushion will be. As you tie one piece of wool to another, leave nice long ends. When your piece of knitting is done, the ends can be trimmed to make small tassels, or tied into little bows that look like little butterflies.

2) Get your knitting needles and begin. If you use size 5 mm needles and thickish wool, cast on 40 stitches. This means your cushion will be about 26 cm wide. If you want a bigger cushion, cast on more stitches. If you want a smaller cushion, cast on fewer stitches.

3) Continue knitting until either:
   a) your wool is finished
   b) you are fed up
   c) your cushion is the right size.

(Remember that you will have to fold your piece of knitting in half and sew it up around the edges to make a cushion, so it will be half the size of the knitting on your needles.)

If you have knitted, say, 40 rows, and can't be bothered to do any more, but want a bigger cushion, then call those 40 rows the front of your Dream Cushion and ask a kind grown-up as pleasantly as you can to knit another 40 rows in a plain colour like cream or grey or beige. You will then have a Dream Cushion with a plain back and a fancy front – which makes no difference to the quality of your dreams.

4) When your cushion is the right size, cast off your knitting.

5) Fold your piece of knitting in half with the inside out and the right side in. Sew round two of the open sides. Leave one side open.

6) Turn the cushion the right way round and fill it up with bits of cut-up tights, etc. Do not fill too full.

7) Sew up the last side as neatly as possible.

8) Put the cushion on your bed, and you will dream about the place you have conjured up in your cushion. THIS IS GUARANTEED. You may not remember the dream in the morning but you will have dreamed it!

Chapter 8
The Otter Street School Christmas Gala

Almost the best hour in the world is five o'clock on a Friday afternoon in December. Outside, it may be dark and cold, but the curtains are drawn against the night, the lamps are lit, Filomena's trampolining is over for the day, and a hush falls over the house until supper-time. It is the perfect hour for napping in the kitchen chair, with fragrant smoke rising from the pots and pans, and the radio burbling in the background.

This particular Friday, however, was different. The house was in a turmoil – that's the only word for it. The reason for this disruption to our normal routine was the Otter Street School Christmas Gala taking place on the Saturday. There wasn't a corner of the house, it seemed, where a cat could settle down. Let me list for you the various activities taking place in 58, Azalea Avenue:

a) *Cooking in the kitchen.*

Rosie was making batches of biscuits and cakes. As one tray of star-shaped (or crescent-shaped or bell-shaped) bits of pale dough went in, another tray of golden biscuits came out. Francesca was helping to pack them into airtight boxes.

'Have you put something special in these?' she said.

'Wait and see,' said Rosie and winked. 'It's going to be quite a Gala. I hope your witch costume is ready.'

Francesca nodded. 'May I borrow Auntie Varvara's evening cape? The black satin one with the silver stars on it?'

Rosie opened the oven door and a wonderful cinnamon smell drifted out. 'If you're careful,' she said. 'Auntie Varvara won't mind. She's in love now, so she won't mind.'

'Don't people mind about other people borrowing their things when they're in love?' Francesca wanted to know.

Rosie said, 'You don't notice much when you're in that state, and you hardly mind about anything.'

Francesca turned to me. 'You must come with me, Ozzy, for the Fancy Dress Parade. Witches always have black cats. You *will* come, won't you?'

I couldn't refuse. Certainly, parading around with a bevy of small children in fancy dress did not befit my age and station, but as I have explained before, I find it hard to say no to Francesca, partly because of my devotion to her, and partly because I had no desire to have my whiskers singed. Furthermore, I had to admit that a witch without a black cat would indeed be a sorry spectacle.

b) *Growing in the greenhouse*

Eddie had lined up almost a hundred jam jars on one of the shelves. 'I've been collecting these jars since last Christmas, Ozzy,' he said. 'It's ever such a good idea. You've seen those huge glass bottles with plants growing in them, haven't you? They cost an awful lot of money and take up such a large space. I'm making small ones, like tiny little gardens in jam jars. 50p each, I'll charge for them, and all the kids'll snap them up. You'll see.'

I was quite sure he was right. Every jar had a pretty arrangement of miniature plants growing in it – ferns and mosses and tiny, tropical-looking leaves. Some even had flowers growing on shrubs no more than half an inch high. It was easy to see why Eddie was so absorbed. It was quite understandable that in all the excitement, neither of us noticed until much later developments that had occurred on the silver branches of the tree grown from the wrappers on tins of fruit. And what were these developments? I shall keep you in suspense for a while longer. It's one of the privileges of being a Narrator.

c) *Persuading Filomena to dress up for her fortune-telling.*

'No one,' said Marco, 'will believe a word you say if you come dressed in a tracksuit.'

'They've turned one whole classroom,' said Bianca, 'into a gypsy caravan.'

Filomena sighed. 'But I'm not consulting the cards or gazing into a crystal ball. I'm knitting, that's all, and seeing what emerges. Mostly it'll just be looking at whoever comes in, and picking up the clues they give away. An awful lot of fortune-telling, of course, is about knowing people. Understanding their needs.'

'But why can't you understand their needs in a gypsy outfit?' Bianca asked.

'Because at my age, I don't feel I have to make a fool of myself.'

'Will you let me be invisible?' asked Marco. 'I'll sit next to you and move things about mysteriously. It'll be very impressive. Perhaps,' he added, 'it will be *so* impressive that no one will notice the fortune-teller's got a purple tracksuit on.'

Filomena put her knitting down. 'Very well,' she said. 'I can see it means a great deal to you. Therefore I shall compromise. I will wear my black silk afternoon frock and my opal brooch. Agreed?'

'Oh yes,' Bianca and Marco said. 'That'll be just right. Thank you, Filomena.'

'I may even,' said Filomena, 'drape a black lace scarf around my head – in for a penny, in for a pound.'

'You'll be the main attraction,' said Marco. 'I can't wait.'

Next morning at breakfast, Filomena made an announcement.

'I've gone into Fair Isle,' she said, 'and you all know what that means.'

'A very busy day,' said Rosie.

'Comings and goings,' said Bianca.

'Toings and froings,' said Marco.

'A bit of this and a bit of that,' said Francesca.

'But lots of fun and excitement,' said Bianca.

'Quite right,' said Filomena, helping herself to more coffee. 'But more important than any of those, an overall harmony of colours and symmetry of pattern that indicates ...'

'... a happy day for everyone!' said Bianca, Marco, and Francesca together.

'Exactly!' Filomena beamed at her grandchildren.

'You children had better help to clear up the

kitchen and pack the van with all our stuff,' said Rosie, 'otherwise we won't be ready in time, and then it'll be a very miserable day, Fair Isle or no Fair Isle.'

'Where is Eddie?' said Filomena suddenly, noticing that her son was absent.

'He's in the greenhouse,' said Marco. 'Shall I go and fetch him?'

'Yes, dear,' said Rosie, and Marco ran out of the room.

'I thought,' said Filomena, 'that Eddie had finished packing his plants and jam jars last night ...'

Francesca had left the table and was looking out of the window. 'He's coming,' she said. 'He's carrying the silver tree. It looks really heavy and it's got funny things all over it.'

Eddie staggered into the kitchen and put the silver tree in its pot down on the floor next to the freezer. 'Now what,' he said, 'do you all think of that, eh?'

No one said anything for a while. We were all, I think, trying to work out what had happened. Francesca came to her senses first.

'Someone,' she said, 'has tied tins all over your tree.'

'They haven't tied them on,' Eddie breathed. 'These tins have grown on to the tree.'

'Nonsense,' said Filomena. 'Tin cans don't grow on trees.'

'Have a look,' said Eddie, standing back to let everyone come closer.

'It's true,' said Rosie. 'There are tins growing out of the branches. It's amazing ... how did you do it?'

'And what's in the tins?' Bianca wanted to know. 'Is there anything in them?'

'There's only one way to find out,' said Eddie. 'Fetch me a tin-opener, Francesca.'

Eddie picked a can from one of the lowest branches. It came away quite easily in his hand. Then he put the tin on the kitchen table and opened it carefully. Everyone came closer to have a look.

'It looks,' said Rosie, 'like a tin of fruit salad.'

'I'll taste it,' said Eddie. He picked up a spoon. 'Peaches, pears, apricots, mandarins, guavas, lychees ...' His eyes opened wide and he turned quite pale and sat down quickly. 'All the fruits whose wrappers I put into this pot.' He stood up. 'I have grown,' he declared, 'the first Fruit Salad Tree in the world!'

He sounded so triumphant that everyone started clapping and cheering. Francesca, Marco, and Bianca started dancing round the table, chanting over and over, 'He's done it! He's done it! A Fruit Salad Tree!'

Rosie said, 'Fetch the lemonade out of the cupboard.'

Filomena said, 'Oh, Eddie, my dear boy, I knew you

had it in you. I did really. I saw yellow for wealth in the knitting only yesterday, only I didn't like to raise anyone's hopes.'

'Are we going to be on TV?' asked Bianca.

Eddie blushed. 'I don't know about that. I mean it is only a tinned Fruit Salad Tree, and not a real one. Still, it's a start. No telling what will happen next. Now come along, everyone, drink your lemonade and let's get moving. We've got a Gala to take part in.'

'But first,' said Rosie, 'I propose a toast. To Eddie, the dad with the greenest fingers in the world.'

'Eddie!' everyone shouted, and drank their lemonade in a gulp.

The Otter Street School Christmas Gala is over. The parents and children who came to it will remember it for many years to come. It was an occasion bathed in sunlight. That was Francesca's doing. The real weather was damp and grey, but over Otter Street School, the clouds had rolled back, and the sun shone out over the school buildings, the playground, and the surrounding streets where all the cars were parked.

Rosie stood behind the cake stall, and sold the cakes that mothers had been busy making for days. She also sold all her biscuits. Most people put their bags of biscuits away to eat later, when they got home, but a few children nibbled them then and there. I watched one or two doing this, and a most extraordinary thing happened. They ran as quickly as their legs could carry them out into the playground and there they began to float and drift and hover, about a foot and a half above the ground. After a while, there were quite a number of people doing this and others watching them, their mouths hanging open in amazement.

'It's almost like flying,' Rosie said to me. 'And it only lasts a few minutes. They become weightless for a while and feel an overwhelming urge to frolic about in the fresh air. It soon passes, and then they just feel happy. And full of delicious biscuit.'

Eddie sold every jam jar garden in the first hour, but his mind was still on the Fruit Salad Tree.

'Wrappers, Ozzy,' he murmured. 'The secret is in the wrappers. We can grow combinations of anything in tins ... think of it.' His eyes grew bright as he contemplated a future full of marvels.

Marco, who had been invisible since lunchtime, thought Filomena looked unexpectedly glamorous in her black dress and scarf. She knitted faster than she had ever knitted before, and when someone came in, she glanced up from her needles and made pronouncements: 'a birth ... a journey ... a quarrel ... a dark stranger ... good news ... good health ... an unexpected gift ... wealth ... a new washing machine ... a letter on Monday morning ... a visitor from abroad.'

Everyone who heard her was most impressed, not least because of Marco's unseen contribution. As Filomena spoke, he picked up this ball of wool or that, and moved them about in the air in patterns – figures of eight and circles. Sometimes he would move two balls of wool at once, tossing them into the air like a juggler and catching them and moving them so that they criss-crossed with one another. Gypsy Filomena (that was what the notice pinned up outside the classroom called her) was an enormous success, and there were soon queues of people waiting in the corridor to have their fortune told and puzzle over the problem of how inanimate objects came to be flying around the room.

Bianca had agreed to help Mrs Dawes on the toy stall.

'It *does* all look a bit shabby, doesn't it?' said Mrs Dawes. 'The trouble is, no one gives toys away until they're thoroughly played with, and by then, well, jigsaws have bits missing, dolls are minus half their clothes, and all the cuddly toys look as though they've been chewed for months on end!' She ran a harassed hand through her hair. 'Your father and mother seem to have sold everything they had, and look at us.'

'It'll be all right,' said Bianca. 'People will come back here later when they've been everywhere else. I can take care of everything if you like, and you can go and have a cup of tea.'

'Honestly?' Mrs Dawes looked much happier immediately. 'I won't be long, but I would love a drink. Will you manage all right?'

'Oh yes,' said Bianca. 'I'll be fine. I expect I'll have sold lots of things by the time you get back.'

Mrs Dawes bounded off in the direction of the canteen.

Bianca turned her attention to the sorry collection of toys piled up in front of her. 'Right, you lot,' she said to them, 'let's get you sorted out.'

By the time her teacher came back, the stall was empty.

'I don't know how you did it, Bianca,' said the astonished Mrs Dawes. 'It's quite miraculous.'

I know how she did it. I actually saw her doing it. Every time a child came up to the stall, Bianca brought something else to life. A little girl saw a tattered old plush giraffe do a dance on the corner of the table.

'I want it, Mummy,' she cried at once. 'Please.'

'It's a bit of rubbish,' said her mother.

'I want it,' said the little girl. 'It's only 10p.'

A boy saw a wooden fire engine drive along the edge of the stall, and four squat little wooden firemen run about with hoses and buckets. He bought it with his last 25p. An elderly teddy bear with one eye missing sang *The Teddy Bears' Picnic* under his breath, a broken train clattered along a plastic track with half the sleepers missing, a collection of finger puppets in the shape of mice squeaked aloud and ran about, and the fluffy ducklings from the picture on one of the jigsaw puzzle boxes waddled in between the few toys still left unsold.

'Oh,' said Bianca when Mrs Dawes returned, 'it was nothing. Honestly.'

She winked at me.

Being a modest Narrator, I have left my own triumph until the end. Francesca and I won first prize in the Fancy Dress Parade, and I like to think that it was my contribution which made all the difference. The judge hesitated for a long time over a rather clever telephone and a very effective pirate, but chose us in the end. There were at least half a dozen other witches, but not one of them had any kind of cat, let alone one like myself. I am not, as readers of this narrative know, one to boast, but I did, I think, give an outstanding performance, contriving to look cosy and sinister at the same time. This, you can rest assured, is no mean achievement. Francesca's prize was a box of sweets and some kind person had found a tin of cat food for me, but the prizes were nothing. What mattered was the honour and the applause, and what was sweetest was Francesca's obvious delight. She carried me round in her arms for the rest of the afternoon.

The Otter Street School Christmas Gala was over. The curtains were drawn against the dark and the whole family was sitting in the lounge, listening to the rain against the window panes.

'Filomena,' Francesca said suddenly, 'will you teach me how to knit, please?'

'I think,' Filomena answered, 'that you're a little young. Perhaps next year.'

Francesca began to look dangerous. 'Please teach me now. I'm sure I could do it. I *want* to do it.'

Filomena put down her own knitting and considered her granddaughter carefully. 'Perhaps,' she said at last, 'you are the one who will inherit. Come over here and I'll show you the beginnings.'

Francesca watched. Then she began to knit, clumsily, slowly, with big, uneven stitches.

'I can do it!' she cried after a while. 'I can knit, and I can tell what's going to happen, just like Filomena, so there.'

'Really?' Eddie smiled. 'Well, tell us then, what's going to happen next?'

Francesca glanced up. 'I'm knitting brown and white. I know what that means.'

'Bet you don't,' said Bianca.

'Bet I do,' said Francesca.

'Go on, then,' said Marco. 'You tell us.'

'It means,' Francesca smiled enigmatically, 'pie and mash for supper!'

'Is that right, Rosie?' asked Filomena. 'Is that what we're having?'

'As it so happens,' said Rosie, 'that's exactly what we're having.'

Filomena nodded and I knew what the nod meant. It meant that the gift, her gift, has been passed on. Francesca will grow up to be someone who knows the patterns and the colours. I have always said that she was someone special and different.

I looked around at the family. Eddie was prodding the earth around his silver tree, dreaming of more and more spectacular combinations of fruit, Rosie was making ticks beside the items she fancied from a glossy catalogue, Bianca and Marco were arguing about whether there was time for a game of draughts before supper, and Francesca was stroking Leopard, who had fallen asleep in front of the fire. Filomena's needles clicked a soothing rhythm, and I closed my eyes and let the smells of supper drift across my face, happy to be part of the fabulous Fantora family.

EXTRACT FROM MY FILES NO. 9:
Telegram from Auntie Varvara.

ENGAGED TO REMO STOP BLISSFULLY
HAPPY STOP WEDDING JUNE STOP
HOME FOR CHRISTMAS STOP
LOVE VARVARA

About the author

I lived in Manchester for many years,
but moved to Cambridge in 2010.
My husband and I have two daughters and three
grandchildren. We used to have a cat, but no longer
do. I enjoy reading, watching TV and knitting.

I loved writing this book. It's the only properly
funny book among the ninety plus titles I've
published since I started in 1976. I don't write
fantasy and my books are often about very
emotional and sometimes sad things, so when I had
the idea for a family with magic powers, I enjoyed
myself a lot. I became Ozzy the cat and it was
wonderful to be an all-knowing narrator.